Don't Bury Me 'Til I'm Dead

Esther Dau

Don't Bury Me 'Til I'm Dead

Robin

ACCENT BOOKS
Denver, Colorado

MEMBER OF
EVANGELICAL CHRISTIAN
PUBLISHERS ASSOCIATION

ACCENT BOOKS
12100 W. Sixth Avenue
P.O. Box 15337
Denver, Colorado 80215

Copyright © 1977 B/P Publications, Inc.
Printed in U.S.A.

Library of Congress Catalog Card Number: 76-50299
ISBN O-916406-61-X

$\mathcal{R}$obin, for a year and a half, kept a diary of her innermost feelings as she revealed in her daily conversations with her Lord her frustrations when, without warning, her illness came to haunt her and her family. She gave this diary to her pastor, Rev. William T. Hays, of Zion Hill Baptist Church, Jonesboro, Georgia. He, with her husband's permission, prepared it for your reading. Some of the names in the diary have been changed to protect the privacy of some individuals.

How This Story Began

By William T. Hays Jr.

Without warning, trouble gripped Robin in a vise-like hold.

Robin first found out about her trouble when she went to her dentist on what she thought would be a routine visit. Instead, the dentist suggested surgery. She still thought this was merely routine until the surgeon announced that he had found a malignancy and suggested more surgery.

Who was Robin?

She was a young, vivacious woman, full of love and desire to live her Christian life to the full. Her husband, Eugene, was more reserved, a quiet, easy-going type. They had two children, Betty and James, and together they formed a happy family. Robin and Eugene worked together remodeling and furnishing a very old house which was becoming a lovely home.

As her pastor, I came to know Robin because of a school teacher co-worker who was a faithful witness. He invited her to come to our church—and she came. She and Eugene were active in our church and I enjoyed their company very much. Then cancer came to haunt them.

For the many months which followed, I found ministering to Robin a rich and rewarding experience. She was so honest and trusting as she shared her innermost feelings.

While Robin went through anguish, depression, questionings, and pain, she still left an indelible impression on the hospital staff, her roommate, and others whom her life touched.

How does a cancer patient feel? What helps? What makes life more difficult?

On the following pages Robin opens her heart and soul to tell you. In these entries in her diary she records her daily conversations with her Lord. In them you can share her faith and desperation, her joy and pathos, her understanding and confusion. May her story, as she wrote it day by day, bless you, whatever your station or situation in life.

May 31, 1974

My neck was operated on two days ago and now I'm home.

Now, that sounds like a happy trip to the hospital, doesn't it? Unfortunately, it wasn't quite like that, 'cause just four months ago I was in the same place with the same disease, cancer!

I'm trying to keep my chin up but sometimes that gets hard to do. I felt about the same this time as I did before when they told me. The windows were still too small to jump out of, and besides, I was one floor closer to the ground and there was just another rooftop to land on. At best I'd have only ended up with two broken legs and a bruised body.

Now I'm home, so I could play multiple choice on which type of suicide would be more suitable. Hanging myself is out of the question—my neck's too sore. Then, of course, there's the blow-your-brains-out method, but that's just o-u-t—out. I can't stand the sight of blood, especially my own. Why waste a bullet when I could just ask someone to blow in one ear and out would come the brains? I'd still be stuck with the cancer and no sense left. I could consider an overdose of pills, but from what I've heard and read, it's a good idea to know what you're taking in order to accomplish what you plan.

By the way, there is another way I can think of—I could smoke myself into a lung cancer, but—like all the above mentioned—it too has a drawback. At the rate the neck cancer is growing the lung cancer would have to get on the ball.

Oh, dear, I forgot one, and you'll have to excuse the spelling— medical terms just aren't my bag. How about serosis of the liver? That presents me with another problem just how long does it take cancer to demolish one's liver? I guess I'll have to drop that one too. After all, who likes a drunk? Not me. I've always found drunks somewhat disgusting.

That shows you what a hyprocite I am. I got sanctimonious about drunks while good-ole-me was calmly hunting an easy and painless way out of all my problems. The Bible says there's a time and a place for all things. I know I should be counting blessings so I'll just go to bed and see if I can't do better tomorrow, since I can't count blessings right now. 12:15 A.M.

June 1

Today I had to escape for awhile, so I went shopping. Mom, Betty [Robin's daughter], and I walked for miles through the mall.

My sister Rini just called and it was so nice to talk with her. The Lord willing she'll be with me this time next week. Tonight I thank You, Lord, that I can count my blessings, joyously. With Your care I have everything and no reason to put on a long face. 12:10 A.M.

June 2

Today was almost completely beautiful. I was surrounded with loved ones. All my family, Mom, Dad, husband, children, even aunts, uncles and cousins. The nice part about family is that I'm lucky in that I can just enjoy being with them. I don't feel compelled to entertain.

I had only one dark spot today and for that I can thank a church member. People who make such blunt, unfeeling remarks still shock me. She started the visit off in bad taste. Number one, she appeared unannounced at lunch time. Number two, she made two uncalled-for remarks to my invited guest. After that, I lost track of the times she put her foot in her mouth. Number three, she overstayed. Then, number four, she took it upon herself to volunteer (and volunteers hadn't been asked for) to inspect my laundry room. I have a thing about displaying dirty rooms to people I don't know too well.

I'm not through yet. Number five, as a parting shot she said, "I'm glad to see you in such good spirits. My father had cancer and when they opened him up he was eat up with cancer. They just closed him back up and didn't give him six months, but he lived for three years." So much for good spirits.

I'm counting blessings again. Thank You, Lord, that I'm not acquainted with many like her. I'm not sure whether it's ignorance or viciousness, but I'll try to remember to pray about it. Then I'll hope to be careful myself about rattling off at the mouth.

It's a real comfort to see loved ones show concern but not act extremely different from the way they've always acted toward me. Naturally it makes me feel good to know people care about me, but I don't want to be treated like some sort of freak. I suppose most people in my situation go through this.

Some of my friends and relatives keep a positive attitude about it, while others (and I'm grateful that these are in a minority) are totally negative. They come at you with this line, "Bless your heart, you poor thing; try to be cheerful." Some even come on hearty and boom at you, "Don't you worry about a thing. You're gonna be fine, just fine."

Isn't that ironic—those were almost the exact words of one of the doctors before he operated and found the second cancer. I'm no fool. They don't know any more than I do about how fine I'm going to be in regards to the cancer. I'll be fine—all right—I just don't know where I'm going to be fine—here or in heaven. One thing I do know, heaven has got to be finer. 11:10 P.M.

June 3

Today was just a Monday. I straightened the house a bit and read a lot. I finished *What a Way to Go* by Bob Laurent. It's a tremendous book; the guy has a realistic view of Christianity. In so many religious books the writers never seem to get across what they feel or think. I guess thinking is one thing while putting it into words is quite another. I should know, sometimes I have to dig around a bit to come up with a suitable word.

Tomorrow I go to Dr. Green to get my stitches out and hopefully get a little information.

Pat Henley, one of my best friends, just called. She is now a grandmother. Her daughter had a baby girl, 8 pounds one ounce. Naturally, she was delighted. Pat is one of my friends that's for real. Her attitude toward me is the same as it was a couple of years ago when she and I were going to adult school together.

She's older than me by twenty-six years but she's one of the best friends I've ever had.

I have two special, special friends—Pat and Sarah. Oddly enough both of them are Mormons. Sarah Hix recently went into the Mormon Church. Sarah was a member of Zion Hill Baptist when we joined. Her husband joined the Mormon Church as a young Christian. I'm afraid Christians fail by not helping new believers build a foundation. I'm ashamed that I don't know more myself, but I do know that I'm very skeptical of a group that uses any book more than the Bible.

Study books are one thing but I personally couldn't accept a mere man's book (Joseph Smith's) as a comparison to God's Holy Bible. I know what God said in Revelation about adding to and taking away from the Bible, so it doesn't make sense that centuries later He'd endow a man with a vision and add to an already perfect book, especially when the addition is not so perfect and just doesn't compare.

I can only hope and pray that my two beloved friends have believed and accepted my Saviour. I'm not hung up on denominations but am hung up on the fundamental truths. I believe there will be people from different denominations in heaven but only if they've accepted Christ as personal Saviour. I'm tired so I'm going to stop for now. 11:25 P.M.

June 5

I didn't write yesterday because I had such staggering blows that I was in shock. I went to a specialist and he didn't paint any rosy pictures. He suggested cobalt treatments and another operation that would make the other one look like a tooth extraction. This one would involve removing part of my tongue, part of my jawbone, plus leaving a big sunken place in my neck. Then after all that, he said there was a 75% chance that cancer would recur.

When he told me that, all I could say was "My God, what a nightmare." I wasn't being disrespectful to God, I was trying to clutch at sanity. My world was reeling around me. I've wondered how other people in my condition felt, but if I had known anybody in a situation like this I wouldn't have asked him. I felt pretty brave last time but I feel terrified this time. I'm trying desperately to get it all together but I feel strongly that I won't be here this time next year unless the Great Physician intervenes. Whatever He has in mind I'm sure He can give me the strength for it. I'm asking him to help me make the right decisions about which course to take. I'm also asking Him to help me keep things as normal as possible around home for everyone's sake. 10:25 A.M.

Hays: *I believe the terminal patient, especially the terminal cancer patient goes through four stages.*

1. *Rejection—not me!*
2. *Rebellion—why me?*
3. *Realization—help me.*
4. *Resignation—oh me.*

Regardless of the suspicions or fears of the patient as he heads toward surgery, nearly everyone rejects the idea that he could really have cancer. He may explain, "The diagnosis is premature"; "All the reports are not in yet"; or "The doctor thinks he got all of it, and it will be a matter of time before we know that for sure."

Soon, while still experiencing this form of rejection, the thought begins to grow, "Why me?" "I'm still young; I have so much to live for; my children need me; my husband could not make it without me."

It was at this point that I found Robin beginning to experience a great deal of depression. The "Why" kept nagging at her, and I could not answer all of her "Why's," nor could anyone else.

June 5

Eugene is fixing lunch. He's holding up beautifully and for that I thank God. I realize that this is a bit much for him, too. God gives amazing strength. While I was sitting in the doctor's office yesterday I kept thinking, I'm going to start screaming and never be able to stop. But the Lord was with me again and I was able to walk out reasonably sane. Lord, You know I won't be able to stay that way unless You take over. I can't do another thing without an abundance of Your care. Maybe this is what You wanted from me all along; I don't seem to be too clear, but I do know I've always had lots of room for improvement.

Suddenly I know that I've wasted a lot of time, but I don't intend to waste any more regardless of how much I have. On the way home yesterday I looked up at the sky and saw beautiful gold-trimmed clouds and wished for a moment that they'd roll back and I'd see You coming. I guess that was selfish, especially when I personally know people that are without Christ. Why couldn't I have seen this without going through all this trouble? Some people (meaning myself) are so stubborn that it takes a mighty blow. 12:05 P.M.

9:35 P.M.

Another day comes to a close and I feel better than I've felt yet. For the first time I talked to Marilyn [her sister] and Mom. I have to admit that I dreaded that, not because I don't love them dearly but because I was afraid they'd go all to pieces and that I couldn't take it. Well, Lord, once more I see Your hand; You gave them strength also. I also came out of my shell and talked to Pat Henley. She made my heart sing for a change. You know I've cried a lot, prayed a lot, and felt despair to the very depths of my soul, but thank You for people like my family and Pat. It's true that sometimes people's lack of feeling leaves me stunned, but on the other hand are those whose love overwhelms me.

Preacher Hays was once more a pillar of strength. He has such a simple way of untangling my jumbled thoughts.

I'm sorry that I've never been able to really talk to pastors that I've had in the past. I'm not completely blaming them because I've never been much on letting people get too close to me. I know you can get hurt by getting close to people, but you can also miss out on some beautiful experiences.

Pat is an example of that. Ordinarily I would avoid someone of a different religion, like the plague, but for some reason I didn't with her. I can't help but feel You had a hand in it, Lord, because she has been a balm to my battered soul more than once. Didn't you use her, Lord? I'm still counting on You to lead me to make the right decision and I'd really like to know if You're leading me. You said ask, Lord, so I'm asking and now I'll wait. You know the whole situation so I'm putting it in Your hands to the best of my ability. 10:15 A.M.

June 6 3:25 P.M.
One of the ladies from the church just left and I enjoyed her visit. It was a nice warm visit—no gloom. Lord, You haven't given me any answers yet concerning my decision but thanks for the inner peace.

Preacher Hays called to let me know he would be gone a couple of days. He also wanted to see how I was feeling. Another example of really caring.

I think Eugene is beginning to get on edge from sitting around not doing much of anything plus all this other. I think now it would be best if he went back to work or he'll end up with his sanity to worry about. We're going to pick up the kids tonight so that should help matters some—it will help things seem more normal. 3:40 P.M.

June 7 8:05 A.M.
I talked to Dr. Skinner and he's going to call the hospital as soon as the office opens. Lord, I still feel against the surgery that the other doctor feels I should have. I don't know yet that's the way You want me to feel or not, but I still know You can handle the situation. I'm much more willing to put myself completely in Your hands as you mentioned in James 5; and I know You can let me know. If it's Your will that I die, I still feel more confidence in You. The doctor said he'd give me a 25% chance. I know he doesn't give me life nor take it away. I know that You sometimes use doctors but I feel I'm past what they can do. My feelings are still somewhat jumbled so, Lord, please continue staying close to me.

We went to Marilyn's last night. We were going to get the kids but decided to leave them another day since I'm still up in the air about seeing another doctor. If You don't want me to see any more doctors, please let me know and I won't.

I don't know how much the kids realize, but Betty did put some questions to me so she must have figured something was wrong. I told her as much as I thought I could without burdening her childish mind. 8:25 A.M.

12:15 P.M.

Heavenly Father, You're the only one who knows the torment my battered soul is going through. Please give me strength. I'm up for a while, then I'm down; how much more can I stand?

> **Hays:** *In this depression, suicide was often in Robin's thoughts. In fact, she talked both with her husband and me about suicide. She made her husband promise not to hide his guns. I feel many cancer patients have thoughts of suicide when they reach the "Why me?" stage.*

6:25 P.M.

Lord, You know I'm like an elevator—up one minute and down the next. Thanks again for the uplift. My husband's mom just called and made me feel so small. She'd heard something about a Cancer Research Foundation in Texas and she offered to send me there and pay expenses. Comfort comes from some of the strangest sources. Is that You again, Lord? When Eugene told me what his mom said, once more my tears overflowed, or maybe my heart overflowed through my tear ducts. His mother and I haven't always been close but for the past five years I've felt close to her. Eugene assured me it wasn't just talk, he said she meant it.

I'm facing another situation—the kids are coming home and now I'll need a double portion of that strength. I'm gonna go ahead and say, "Thanks, Lord," 'cause I know You're ready and waiting. I know that those down moments are compliments of lucifer (I refuse to capitalize his name). He'd like nothing better than to step in and totally wreck my self-control. 7:10 P.M.

I want to run away and yet it's all I can do to walk.
Sometimes I feel the urge to wrap myself in silence
and cease
to talk.
Do I feel sorry for me, you bet I do.
Superhuman I'm not, of that type I've met few.

June 9 9:00 P.M.

I didn't write yesterday; it was a full and happy day. My sis, Rini, flew in last night and we picked her up at the airport about eleven. We talked until about two this morning. Mom and Dad came down today. Of course, they wanted to visit with Rini, too. I'm so glad she came.

9:30 P.M.

I talked with Preacher Hays and each time I talk with him, Lord, You seem even nearer to me. It really pains me to know that we Christians miss out on so much by not being closer. How many times have I neglected to be of help to another soul when I could have been. Lord, help me to be what I should be, now more than ever. I realize people are watching me (and it ain't too comfortable). Help me not to be a disappointment or a let-down to someone.

It's almost unreal the way I feel most of the time. Now, Lord, You know I don't know the future but three-quarters of the time I feel good. Thanks. I wish I were more eloquent, but then again maybe I wasn't meant to be. I'd probably be so high and mighty nobody could stand me, least of all You. Lord, why didn't I think to ask the doomsday predicting doctor, if he knew the Great Physician? I'm sorry I think so slowly, Lord, I don't know if You plan to heal me or not, but if not I do know You'll do a great body transplant. I'm not being flip, but right now I feel like shouting. Believe me, I know shouting praises are better than the feeling of wanting to scream in terror; I've felt both.

Lord, You know I'm a somewhat dramatic creature, I've even had the audacity to feel anger when I hear other people laugh. How's that for wallowing in self-pity? We'll have to watch me, huh? When people say nice things to me, I'm at a loss what to reply. I do know the nice things are the part of me that You handle and Robin gets the credit for the ugly part. The thing that's really bad is that I'm inclined to prefer taking the credit that I should give to You. Thanks for each moment. 10:55 P.M.

June 10

I hope I never again forget to say "Thank You, Lord," but I probably will. This is one time I'm not forgetting. Eugene and I both felt You there. Thanks for that peace. Today's trip to the doctor was quite different from last week's. This doctor didn't promise roses either, but Lord, we felt he had compassion. He said he didn't feel that we would gain anything by more surgery. Now, Lord, You know I'd have liked for them to have said, "There's been a terrible mistake. Nothing is wrong." But I rejoice that what he did say was nothing like last time.

I also know that in fine health You couldn't use me because I never made myself that available. How many times have I been a disappointment to You? I'm sorry, Lord. I talked to Preacher Hays last night. Now I'm not dense and I know You know about the conversation, but it helps me to put it down on paper. I do want to know about that chapter in James and I still want to talk with the pastor about it.

I'm afraid this is just another one of those places where my ignorance of Your Word shows up. I don't know that much about it. I felt good in the doctor's office and felt that was Your presence. Now, Lord, I want to be honest. There's the possibility that I felt good because he said what I'd rather hear and if that's so, I'll rely on You to reveal to me whatever You do want me to do. Lord, I feel so good. What a waste! Thirty years old and I could have felt Your nearness many times, but I missed out by trying to be so self-reliant. 8:30 P.M.

> Many times I've sought help in the wrong places,
> Looking for help in man's words and smiling faces.
> To my distress what I looked for wasn't there.
> I cried out to man, "Listen to me, help me, just care!"
> That wasn't enough; I needed comfort and peace within.
> What I reached for comes from God, not men.

June 11 8:50 P.M.

Well, Lord, today started the treatment. I was scared but You were there. I never knew I was such a coward. I saw the many people who were there for different types of treatment and in different areas of the body. I was surprised to see that I wasn't the only young person there. Has my head been in the sand, like an ostrich? Did I really think things like this only happened to the aging? So what if you're 10 years, 30 years, 50 years, or 80 years old? No one's exempt because of age.

I've heard fear in conversations, not in what was said but in tones. I've seen it in faces, and plenty of times when I have glanced in the mirror I've seen it there. I've even heard it in laughter. Thanks to You, Lord, I've known terror, despair and blessed peace, all in a matter of seconds.

How's this for a good verse? "In God have I put my trust: I will not be afraid what man can do unto me" (Psalm 56:11).

Lord, I was embarrassed today about that scripture I was quoting to myself. I didn't get too far before I flat gave out. I saw what a mess I'd be in if suddenly I didn't have access to the Bible. Lord, help me to express myself clearly when I tell others about this. I really need Your help because there's enough confusion in the world without my adding to it. Lord, help me not to be paralyzed by fear of life, death, pain, or by what people might think of me. 9:25 P.M.

Hays: *After a while, especially as health deteriorates, or additional treatment is required, the patient may begin to accept the reality of the disease and its final result. Robin did! "OK," she said, "Cancer, c-a-n-c-e-r. SAY IT!"*

June 12 7:28 P.M.

Today was the second day of treatment. I was tremendously nauseated this morning but they tell me that doesn't have anything to do with the treatments. The nurse said it was just nerves. I got to feeling pretty rough this afternoon. I suppose I may have overdone things—we went shopping at the mall. Or the way I feel may be from the nausea that I've had all day.

19

The doctor told me to follow my normal routine. Maybe I should have told him something about my normal routine. I may have to slow up a bit.

Hays: *After the surgery Robin had continued to work as a teacher's aid in one of the local elementary schools.*

Lord, I don't feel all that nervous but it may just be a build-up of the strain of last week and You know about that. I'm so thankful for all that You have done for me, especially the beautiful peace that You've seen fit to give me when I needed it the most. They told me today that the paint would have to stay on my face. Help me not to be silly about it.

10:15 P.M.

Lord, I've debated about taking the kids to the clinic with me— You know it exposes them to quite a bit and I'm not too sure about that. James had another round of walking in his sleep again. This usually happens when he's been upset about something. I know children can't be shielded from everything but I believe over-exposure is a large problem of the kids today. Does an adult have the right to snatch these precious years away from them? I'm tired once more and must go to bed.

June 13 9:25 A.M.

Once again I await treatment at the clinic. Some of the sights I see tear my heart out. Maybe all adults should be exposed to a bit more of this. It puts me to thinking, not to mention looking heavenward.

I've been reading the book on James that Preacher Hays brought by. It pretty much says what I've been taught—Daddy had said the same things. Anyway it's reassuring to be refreshed on some things that I had forgotten.

Lord, I don't want to start listening to people—in general they have a tendency to frighten me. How do I stay civil and tell them I don't want to hear some of the things they say? Lord, help me to be stronger in faith. I know it's wrong to worry and I'm trying like

I've never tried before.

3:40 P.M.
Rini went to Mom and Dad's for supper. She took Betty with her so that she wouldn't have to drive back alone. When she's here the house rings with her laughter. I hope she's as happy as she appears to be. Sometimes I think she's much like me, and then again I wonder.

Lord, forgive us when we become guilty of "everything's hopeless" (especially me). 4:00 P.M.

The Hansons (a couple from church) came by and visited a while tonight. It was a nice visit.

June 14 4:25 P.M.
Rini took the kids and walked up to the big town of Jonesboro. Eugene is working so this is one of the few times I've been alone. I think the family is wanting to hover over me and that's fine as long as they don't expect me to be laughing all the time. I'm sorry, Lord, but I just can't manage that—it's not my nature.

I guess this cancer bit is about as rough on the loved ones as it is on me. If they're too cheerful I'm wary and if they're dreary I think they're burying me. Lord, help me to strike a happy medium.

I feel somewhat tired today; maybe I'm the one that's dreary.

This is weird but I have the hiccups a lot.

June 15 10:45 P.M.
Rini left with Marilyn and her kids tonight. In the morning they will all fly to Louisiana. Rini is taking them with her for a little vacation. Lord, please watch over them all, especially Marilyn and Sue since they seem more anxious.

I was happy to see Rini and she was very helpful in getting me started with my treatments. I'll miss Marilyn but hope she enjoys her trip. I'll miss Rini too, but I'm used to her being away.

Well, Lord, I read what James said about healing and three other books concerning what James said. How's this for stupidity? Now I'm not positive about how I should pray about the matter. My life would have been less complicated if I'd been born a dog, or some other animal. I guess I've got just enough sense to blow my mind. Right about the time I think I have something down pat, along comes something else. You gave me a brain, Lord, and I am getting confused. Lord, help me to do what You'd have me to do and pray in the manner that will please You.

You know the last several Sunday School lessons that I taught my three-year-olds have been about healing. That just struck me tonight! Funny, I hadn't thought about that before. Maybe with all my company and everything I haven't had time to get my thoughts together. I know one thing—if I'm healed there will never be any doubt about who did it.

The first day I went in for treatments, one of the machines was being worked on. That sure doesn't make me want to rely on one of their machines. It's an odd feeling, lying on that bed watching that machine being lowered to my neck, then seeing the nurse get out of there pronto, before she turns it on. I'm glad You're with me always. I'd hate to think I was at the mercy of an *unpredictable* machine. It's true! I don't always understand what you tell me through Your Word or the Holy Spirit, but I do understand the failures are on my part, not Yours.

Preacher Hays came by today. Today was another one of those times when I felt unable to collect my thoughts well enough to reach him. I'm glad You know when I'm reaching out, Lord, and even more glad that it's not always imperative that I use specific words to make You understand. 11:45 P.M.

June 16 10:25 P.M.

I went to church tonight, red mark on my neck and all. I know I'm silly about it but I haven't overcome things like that, yet. I honestly don't mind being different when it comes to some things but there are different kinds of different. Today is Father's Day but we didn't go visiting. I was tired and needed to rest. I spent the time reading, listening to Jack Holcomb's records and thinking. Eugene worries when I'm quiet, but, Lord, You know I need time to think things out.

Tomorrow starts the second week of treatments. The more I

go, the closer I need You, Lord. If I went in with my eyes closed and my mind blank I wouldn't dread going so much. I guess I'd like to pretend things like this don't happen to anyone. How does a person get to be my age and know so little? Even so, I wouldn't recommend that everyone be awakened the way I was.

Sometimes I don't feel real. So often I feel remote and apart from people and situations. I've always felt this way to a certain degree but never more so than now. Eugene says I'm going into a shell. Maybe so. After all, how much can you say? Cancer is not easy to dismiss. 11:00 P.M.

June 17

I had planned on driving this morning but at the last minute I asked Eugene to take me. Last night I dreamed he was murdered and woke up feeling uneasy. I had a nightmare night before last too. I wonder if my frame of mind is causing my subconscious to make me dream like that. 8:55 A.M.

Waiting Room 9:30 A.M.

I look about me and feel slightly amused that this room is called a "waiting room." Waiting for what? Perhaps an extension to one's life span, waiting for pain to be relieved, or what? I see so many elderly people in such miserable fixes that I wonder about desperately hanging on to life.

Lord, sometimes I feel like I've lived ten years in the last two weeks. While I was waiting, a lady commented that the room had such pretty wallpaper. If anyone had asked me I couldn't have guessed its color. I'd probably have said gray.

8:25 P.M.

I talked to Edward on the phone and he commented on my bravery. Lord, what makes people think I'm brave? I wasn't offered a whole lot of choices and You and I both know that at the time suicide was the most attractive. That's not being brave, but you don't go around discussing that possibility with the average healthy American. I'm scared every time I lie down on that bed and watch that enormous machine come down to my neck. Maybe it's not so enormous but that's the way it looks to me. If I didn't know You were there I'd flee in horror.

I'm listening to Jack Holcomb sing "Ship Ahoy!" I thought these words described me:

> And the Captain's kind ear, ever ready to hear,
> Caught my wail of distress, as I cried out in fear:
> Ship ahoy!

Then the other song was "Balm in Gilead."

> There is a Balm in Gilead
> To make the wounded whole.

Thanks again, Lord, I'm sure Jack Holcomb is with You now. Lord, would You mind delivering a message? Tell him the voice You gave him and the way he used it has been a blessing to me so many times that I'd have lost count several years ago, if I'd have counted.

Eugene and I have had some interesting conversations on faith. It might be interesting to get twenty definitions of faith in regards to healing, ten from supposedly healthy people and ten from seriously ill people. Perhaps we use the word "faith" too lightly. I think I'm getting too deep for me. I'm afraid once more I must seek soothing sleep. Lord, help those who are unable to sleep. 10:20 P.M.

June 18

I seem plagued with bad dreams. Why, Lord? Does it soothe the body when we sleep and have such terrible dreams? I woke nauseated. They say it's nerves but I don't know. At any rate I couldn't take a valium because I knew I'd be driving.

10:00 P.M.

Today was a good day. I've felt happy. Thanks, Lord. I still feel torn apart when I see the people at the clinic because I see so much hopelessness. God, please help me to be of help if I can. Today I got weighed and the doctor checked my neck. He questioned me about side effects but I'm really unsure about what symptoms are side effects and what I'm supposed to chalk up to nerves.

This is the way I feel: nauseated frequently, hiccups frequently, my mouth is sore, my mouth is dry, I have some trouble swallowing, my throat is getting sore, I'm already losing my desire to eat, losing taste and oftentimes very tired, whether I've done anything much or not. My weight is about the same so far.

Lord, be with the nurses and doctors. Give them strength to care without being torn apart, and that kind of strength can only come from You. 10:50 P.M.

June 19

Mrs. Hanson came by again today and I really enjoyed the visit. It amazes me, the people I never got to know when I was well. She's an interesting person. I enjoy listening to her as well as talking to her. She is a very perceptive person. Lord, I'm thankful for people like her. She sensed my distress over the prayer situation and promptly brought it before You when she prayed as she was leaving. Help me to be more observant, for I have a habit of wandering off in my mind and not even listening. It really makes me ashamed when I meet someone like her. I feel so much better when I'm not wrapped up in me.

10:13 P.M.

I went to church tonight and didn't feel like anyone was staring. Thanks, Lord. I had actually thought I should go in hiding for six weeks. Sometimes I try to express my deepest feeling to someone and I bomb out. Either I'm not being clear or they don't want to hear. Are people afraid to listen? Sometimes I think that they think if they really listen, then they will somehow get involved and therefore be in danger. I know that there have been times when I'd close my mind rather than find out about something that was frightening.

Lord, forgive me for feeling fright so often rather than completely trusting. I know it's not good to be wishy-washy but I've never been thrown such a staggering blow. How long is it gonna take me to get it all together? I'm tired now. . .I must stop and try to rest. 10:35 P.M.

June 20 9:15 A.M.

Once again in the waiting room. This must be the coldest hospital I've ever been in. I wear long sleeves and still I'm cold. I'm beginning to know most of the faces and now most of them are older than me, in years that is. Sometimes now I feel more than ancient. I slept good last night—no bad dreams. Thanks, Lord. 9:20 A.M.

June 20 5:25 P.M.

Guess what? I'll just tell, 'cause no one would guess. The nurse took a picture of my neck today. Isn't that eerie? I asked, "Why the picture?" She said, "For the records in case it should ever come up in court."

Why even mention having a good positive attitude? When I'm a physical wreck my mental stability is questionable, to say the least. Lord, I think it would be nice if we fooled them all. Naturally you'd have to do the healing—all I've got is a sick body and enough sense to know that You're quite capable. I'm not trying to bargain, I don't have anything to bargain with. It wouldn't work anyway. You know me too well.

> **Hays:** *During this time Robin began to ask about healing, faith or otherwise, miracle drugs, untried drugs, rumors, whatever...anything, as she grasped for a straw of hope to live. This doesn't mean that she lost her faith in God. She never lost that. But she did have a strong desire to live, and was willing to try anything to keep living.*
>
> *Somewhere in this stage, the fourth R, Resignation or the "Oh me," comes in. For Robin this was a resignation to the will of God for her life. She could accept healing (Who couldn't?), but she could also accept dying if that was what God had for her.*

9:30 P.M.

Lord, only You know how tired and weary I'm getting and this is only the second week. I know everybody will get tired of hearing me complain and I try not to but it's so hard. I'm honestly grateful for the times that I feel good but when I feel so bad it gets hard to remember how it was when I felt good. I know back in January I thought I'd never feel good again, but You were there and I eventually got over that. Here it is June and I'm dragging rock bottom again. Please be near and make me feel Your presence. Help me to remember this verse I found in Psalm 55:22: "Cast thy burden upon the Lord, and he shall sustain thee: he shall never suffer the righteous to be moved." 9:45 P.M.

June 21 11:25 A.M.

Preacher Hays went with me to the clinic today. It was great. I probably talked his ear off, but it's good to be able to be open with people. There are so few people that I can talk to. It hasn't taken me long to discover that being open with most people gets you weird glances or that pity thing again.

If there is to be any pity floating around I'd rather go off by myself and pity myself in privacy. It surprises me quite a bit that I can talk to the Preacher so easily.

I found it amusing when a little old lady sat down by me and said, "I've been wanting to tell you for a week that you don't have to put up with that red paint on your face. I went home and cried a week when they did that to me. Then I raised Cain and they started using the invisible paint on me."

I know about the invisible paint, but the nurse had told me that it wasn't as good because it wiped off and it made it harder to get the cobalt in exactly the right spot. Ah, well, I don't enjoy the red paint but I can't imagine crying a week over paint on my face.

Lord, do I have a forbidding attitude about me? That lady said it took her a week to get up courage to come to me. Do I look like such a grouch? Maybe I ought to work on my facial expressions.

I've seen some sad sights but today I heard a sad sound, an elderly lady screaming. Sad is not a very good word but it's the best I can do right now. I've wondered a lot about how far a person should go to extend life. Unfortunately, I haven't come up with any magic clues or divine answers. I have so very much to be thankful for. What a shame I don't remember more often.

The book *But God* (by V. Raymond Edman) that Mrs. Hanson brought me is very good, very appropriate. When she mentioned

27

me taking her Sundy School class sometime or giving my testimony, I nearly fell out of my chair. Who me, an adult class? I've always envied people that give such beautiful testimonies, or tell such super fantastic conversion experiences. I've even caught myself wishing I'd waited until I was an adult and had committed some sins that I could tell about, that wouldn't sound funny to adults.

I know children can and do sin but you don't compare sticking out your tongue behind your mother's back to being saved from drug addiction. I understand that the different experiences don't make a person less saved. I'm probably acting silly again because I wouldn't have wanted my own children to put off being saved in order to have super experiences. 2:15 P.M.

7:50 P.M.

Mom over and over told us that a man is only as good as his word. The Preacher kept his once more today. For the first time I flew. I've been apprehensive about flying all my life. The very thought scared me, so I never did fly. I've been scared by so many things this year, that while listening to the Preacher talk about flying back in January I decided I'd like to try it, that I wasn't afraid anymore.

I've missed a lot! I enjoyed every moment, from the takeoff to the landing. If one is going to fly, what better pilot than a preacher? It gave me such a relaxed, dreamy feeling. Do the angels feel so peacefully relaxed, floating here and yonder?

I thought, too bad I can't hop in a plane and fly straight to heaven nonstop and no round trip ticket. Today has been a beautiful day for me from the beginning 'til now. I'm not having any days without physical pain but I still feel joy too. I felt joy looking out of the plane window; it was a different view of Your creation. Thanks again, Lord. 8:20 P.M.

June 22 6:00 P.M.

I'm feeling rough again. The doctor told me I'd have a sore throat. Lord, You know I've had some awful sore throats but this tops them all. It hurts to swallow anything, even my own saliva, and I don't have much of that. It also hurts when my throat is dry. I haven't figured out which is worse.

I'm listening to one of Jack Holcomb's records again. I find them so comforting. It's odd, they comfort me and they make Eugene uneasy. He said the music reminded him of what he thought music would sound like in heaven. Maybe he thinks I'm on my way. I feel halfway there just listening. The way I feel physically, sometimes I wish I were there. It's not that I don't love my family and friends, but I have these times of feeling so bad.
6:30 P.M.

10:00 P.M.

Marilyn and family came by so I had to stop writing. Jack had just picked her up at the airport. They had a lovely flight and enjoyed the trip. Marilyn got the record by J. Holcomb with "After" on it.

> After the toil and the heat of the day,
> After my troubles are past,
> After the sorrows are taken away,
> I shall see Jesus at last.

Talk about heavenly! Rini bought me a beautiful leather Bible. Lord, I know all of them in the family love me and want to do for me, but somehow give them the assurance that I don't doubt for one minute their love or concern. They don't have to buy presents for me—just being themselves is more than enough. If I died tomorrow there's not a one who would have any justifiable reasons for feeling any sort of guilt or regrets concerning their relationships with me.

Poor Eugene, he's the one to be pitied. Now get this. I'm not always polite and nice, and unfortunately he gets the brunt of my ugly side. He should be awarded a medal. Under the best of circumstances I'm not an easy person to get along with and this year hasn't been the best of circumstances.

It hasn't been easy for the kids either. I hope Betty enjoys camp next week. I need to spend some time with James when I'm feeling better. I have times of not feeling so rough and then

I usually run around doing other things. I'll have to let some things slide and spend time with James.

Thank You, Lord, for the many Christians whose lives have touched mine this year. They have so many times been tremendous sources of comfort. 10:40 P.M.

June 23 2:30 P.M.

The swallowing situation got so rough that I went ahead and called the doctor. He gave me some new medicine. He said I should see him before I took my treatments tomorrow. Lord, help me to rely on your promises and not press panic. I went to church this morning but was pretty uncomfortable.

June 24 11:10 P.M.

I've been pretty sick all day today. I'm having trouble keeping food down. They switched my treatments—five days a week instead of four, giving a smaller dosage. Marilyn and her family came tonight;they are going to stay a few days.

June 25

Today has been a far cry from the last three or four days. For a change I've felt human once more. For a while I was beginning to wonder. What was that, Lord?" "Oh ye of little faith?" My apologies, once more.

Marilyn has been stuffing my face every chance she gets. The doctors would be surprised if I gained weight instead of losing it. They don't know Marilyn, or the rest of the family for that matter.

Thanks, Lord, for so much. You've been so close. Help me to be ever mindful of Your presence. I want to be available when I have a chance to be of service. Please, Lord, help me to recognize opportunities and let myself be guided.

June 26 4:05 P.M.

I haven't done much of anything but lie around. I don't seem to have an excess of energy. If I don't take the tablets the doctor gave me, I'm in a lot of pain and discomfort, but if I do take them, I'm so out of it that it's not at all funny. The pain tablets seem to affect my vision. I had that trouble in the hospital. Everything looks double. Then I stagger—and if that's not enough I still have the hiccups. People will think I've been on a week-long drunk.

4:40 P.M.

Eugene and Jack left to go to Florida for a couple of days to go deep sea fishing. I hope they have a nice trip. Eugene really needs it. All this has been quite a mental strain on him too. Maybe he can put it all out of his mind and relax. I plan a trip myself as soon as the treatments are over. I don't know when I've ever felt so drained of energy. When I go on my trip I'm going to need extra attention from You, Lord, because I don't want to dwell on cancer after the treatments are over. I want Your help then as now, each moment as it comes. Looking back often makes one stumble over what's ahead.

June 27 10:35 P.M.

By now, like on most days I feel rough. Lord, I'm beginning to wonder about the treatments. I'm starting to feel that they are killing me. Forgive me for complaining. Sometimes I can't seem to help myself. Help me to remember to rely on You. The physical part is bad enough but the uncertainties involved in the mental part are enough to terrify me to the very depths of my being. That's what it's all about; right, Lord? When I feel myself starting to panic, then I feel You come closer. Thanks for the peace that I can't get elsewhere. I keep remembering that Your Word says in Psalm 55:22, "Cast thy burden upon the Lord, and he shall sustain thee; he shall never suffer the righteous to be moved." Thank You for this comfort. 10:55 P.M.

June 28

I caught up on some of my lost sleep on the way to the hospital. I feel somewhat better this morning. Both Marilyn and I have been amazed at the way James and Sue [Marilyn's daughter] have played together this week. They've spent hours on the front porch counting cars. How's that for entertainment? 10:00 A.M.

The doctors, nurses and personnel here are super people. They are compassionate plus pleasant without seeming phony. Some people are destined to put on that jolly, "ho, ho" act. I've learned to spot them and avoid them. Nine out of ten are the ones who make those shockingly insensitive remarks. I believe that those are the people who are the most terrified of the disease. They're probably thinking about themselves so much that they don't actually think about what they're saying. I can halfway understand people like that but it doesn't alter the fact that I'd rather not be around them. 11:50 A.M.

7:30 P.M.
Today has been a happy-go-lazy day. I haven't fought sleep, for when I felt it coming on I just took a nap. I've felt much better today than I have all week, less pain and discomfort. I feel awfully lazy doing next to nothing. Maybe I should ask about some vitamins.

June 30 3:45 P.M.
I didn't go to church today. I awoke with an awful headache and throwing up once again. If I could figure out a way to avoid going to sleep at night, then I might not feel so bad in the mornings. After the first hour in the morning it's not so terrible—not great, but not terrible.

Here it is the last day of June. I can hardly believe this past month. It still seems so unreal. It's true I often feel pain and discomfort, but on the other hand I feel peaceful much of the time.

Eugene and Jack got in yesterday evening. They enjoyed their trip. I'm glad they got the chance to go.

I haven't slept as much today as I have been doing. I've taken less of the pain medicine so I suppose that's why. When I don't take the pain medicine it makes it very difficult to swallow.

Today a young negro shot Martin Luther King's mother as she played the organ. They've had first one person then another on television about the shooting. We've heard all about the tragedy of the situation. Yes, I, too, can see tragedy but I can also see that she was fortunate. She had already raised her children, she'd already lived a good while, her death was without warning, quick, and she was doing what she enjoyed doing. Maybe that sounds like I'm feeling sorry for myself and maybe I am, but if I could select a way of departing this world and heard about hers, I'd say, "What a way to go." 8:05 P.M.

10:20 P.M.

Mrs. Hanson brought me some more books to read. I really appreciate her going to the trouble to get books for me and coming by so faithfully. So many people dismiss you rather quickly. I should know, I've been guilty of it myself. Lord, I'm sure enough grateful that everybody's not like me.

July 1 5:35 P.M.

I couldn't believe it—I gained two pounds this week. I weighed 109 last week. Marilyn did a pretty good job of feeding me last week. The food business is unbelievable. I can just barely taste three-fourths of the foods I can eat. Usually the ones that I can eat have a peculiar taste.

The pain medicine doesn't help as much now as it did at first, because I'm having trouble swallowing again. I guess I'm getting immune to it. My neck is feeling very stiff now and sore, and some of my hair is coming out on the left side. It's coming out on the underside and not yet noticeable. How many agonies do I have to endure? At this very moment my throat feels like it's closing. I guess it's silly to worry about some hair falling out, but I do. Lord, Lord! 6:25 P.M.

July 2 9:00 A.M.

I feel better than usual this morning and I haven't taken any medicine. Thanks, Lord. This is the first morning in I don't know how many that I haven't spent the whole morning either throwing up or feeling like I was going to. I should have asked for Your help sooner. Babs called this morning, wanting to know if I was going to Marilyn's for the rest of the week. Remind me, Lord, to appreciate special friends.

9:25 A.M.

I've spent quite a bit of time in this waiting room. I'd like to have watched faces but people in here have too many problems already without my adding to their discomfort by staring. I don't know if that's weird curiosity or not.

Dwaine and Jane came last night. I think Jane wanted me to go into detail about how I felt when the doctors told me about the cancer. She was talking about what she might or might not do. She said she didn't think she'd want anyone to know. I don't know how she figures that she could keep it a deep, dark secret.

I'll play the game of "if" with her, now that she's gone. Number one, "if" she lived, it would be too great a miracle to keep quiet about. I don't know why, but with some people I can go into details about the way I feel while with others it's just not smart to even try. I think it has something to do with whether or not that person can listen to what you're saying. 9:50 A.M.

July 3

We're at Marilyn's now. I guess she'll take me to the doctor again this week. I felt good yesterday, all day. Today I hardly finished my coffee and applesauce before I was throwing up. I forgot to ask Your help on this, Lord. By the time I take the nausea medicine and the pain tablets I might as well get ready to sleep. After taking the two, that's all I can do. Needless to say I didn't feel good today.

July 4 11:00 P.M.

No treatment today—holiday. Marilyn's cat celebrated by having kittens. She and I watched them being born. Fascinating. This is truly a fantastic world You created, Lord. As I watched the mother cat having three babies, one right after the other without any help, I was amazed. There's so much we take for granted.

Mom and Dad came out and spent the afternoon. I've felt pretty good most of the day. The eating situation is getting pretty rough. I can't eat anything without a certain amount of pain. Lord, help me not to be a grouch. 11:10 P.M.

July 5 10:00 P.M.

I asked for a different kind of pain tablet since the other one didn't seem to help much. The doctor gave me another prescription but it's less help than the first one. I won't be gaining any weight at this rate. I gained weight only to lose it. We came home tonight but probably just for the weekend. I don't feel well enough to fix meals and keep a household running. We'll probably go back to Marilyn's house next week.

I'm very tired now so I'm going to bed. Isn't it strange, my vocabulary seems to be getting limited to "I'm tired and I don't feel good"? I'm looking forward to better days. 10:10 P.M.

July 6 8:35 P.M.

As usual I'm tired and I don't feel good. I'm getting rather nervous and strung out. Right now it would probably be good if I could stay by myself. It's sad to feel the need to be alone and yet be physically unable to take care of myself. Eugene and the kids are loud and noisy by nature and with my nerves this is a bit much. I just want peace and quiet, but I guess that's asking too much.

It's sad to spend almost half my life married to Eugene and not understand him, nor him me. I ask myself how can this be so, but I know it is. I've heard a lot of people say that this isn't uncommon, but I still think it's awful. Surely one should know a person pretty well after 15 years. If not, then what happens? Lord, help me to be more understanding. Lord, help me to avoid being so self-centered. 8:55 P.M.

> I reached out and life was slipping away.
> Suddenly I was filled with indecision, whether to go or stay.
> This I knew required strength like I'd never possessed.
> I thank the Lord, He supplied as I confessed.
> Out of despair, once more I felt the healing balm,
> I can't explain how but I miraculously felt the calm.
> He calmed the stormy seas and saved those so dear.
> What have I to dread, can He not conquer fear?
> Now once more I'm wrapped safely in His love so strong.
> Life on earth is now, not days or months
> that could be short or long.

July 7 7:15 P.M.

This afternoon Mrs. Hanson brought me some more books and collected some that I had finished. She even brought me some vitamins. The lady amazes me. I'm really thankful for other Christians. It's too bad that most Christians don't know the meaning of true fellowship. Unfortunately, most think it concerns eating and socializing instead of bearing and sharing one another's burdens. Most of us don't even want to hear about another's troubles, much less bear their burdens. I know this is true because when I look back to see too many times that I closed my ears and turned my back. God forgive me. 7:55 P.M.

9:20 P.M.

When I flick back through the pages that I've written since I went back into the hospital I see a lot of mood switching. Not more than normal I hope. I find myself feeling bad physically and good mentally or vice versa. Occasionally I feel bad both physically and mentally at the same time—but not often. More and more I find myself turning to You, Lord. Maybe that's as it should have been all along. 9:50 P.M.

July 8 7:45 P.M.

Thanks, Lord, another good day. The days slip by so quickly. Already I'm going into the fifth week of treatments but it only seems like a couple of days ago that I was in the hospital and they were telling me for the second time—cancer. I've lived a second lifetime since then.

The daylight hours are rapidly turning to darkness and I realize You've blessed me with another day overflowing with Your loving care. Few people could be loved as much as I've been loved in 30 years. The really odd thing about it is that I've never been particularly loveable. 8:00 P.M.

Lord, only You can understand why I say I'm frightened. I'm glad You're there when I come running. More and more I understand why You talk about the earthly family to teach us about how to feel about You. A child is frightened and he runs to his parents. I know and understand that now.

So many times I could have felt Your loving protection but when I felt so sure of myself, I didn't turn to You. Now I *know* I can't depend on my body. I never actually could, but now I've been made to realize it because of the disease. Sometimes I feel so tired, Lord. Please give me the strength to keep going. Often it's hard to carry on in a normal manner. Sometimes I want to scream. My world has turned flip-flops in the last few weeks. Why should I act normal as if nothing's happened?

Most people believe that they'll grow old and then die. When you know that's not likely for you, you're bound to do some thinking. I'm glad You're there to balance things out. 10:50 P.M.

July 9 10:40 P.M.

Today has been a bit rough as my throat has been more sore than usual. I was sick a good bit during the night and that causes a strain on my throat.

Babs called tonight and she's loaded with problems. I want to help her but I'm at a loss as to how I can help. Lord, You know the situation, please give her strength and courage. 10:55 P.M.

July 10 8:05 P.M.

I felt so much better today. If it weren't for the good days I don't think I could make it. I'm forever thankful to have someone take over for me. Naturally I mean Marilyn and Mom. Many people, Babs for an example, don't have anyone that they can turn to. I'm truly blessed for I didn't even have to ask for help.

If I can take each day as it comes I'll be fine, Lord, please help me not to be wrapped up in me. 8:15 P.M.

July 11 10:30 P.M.

The whole neck treatment stopped today. From now until I finish they will only treat the lump. The nurse said I'd have seven more treatments. I haven't felt well today. Finally this evening I used the medicine for nausea which I only take as a last resort because it makes me so sleepy and sluggish. Then everybody seems a long ways away from me. They also sound louder. I was very disappointed about the treatments taking longer. Oh, well, I wasn't promised continuous roses. 10:40 P.M.

July 12 9:10 A.M.

Today is Friday and we'll be going home. Marilyn's house seems like another home because I'm perfectly at ease here. It's really a home away from home. I doubt if many people can say that and really mean it. If I stay home next week it will seem strange. 9:15 A.M.

July 13 10:15 P.M.

Today started off great—then gradually deteriorated. I didn't wake up sick. I drank a cup of coffee, ate a bowl of oatmeal and was feeling fine. Then I started downhill about two o'clock and felt rotten until about seven o'clock. That's the way my days go. Mom and Dad came down this afternoon, but I'm afraid I wasn't too entertaining.

I'm reading a book on Satan—very interesting. It's strange that I haven't read very much on Satan. A lady from the church brought the book by. Why now, Lord? If there's a reason for everything that happens, then why that book now? It sure would simplify my life if You'd just call me on the phone or send me a letter, Lord. I'm tired and soothing sleep beckons. Thank you, Lord, for restful nights.

July 14 10:45 A.M.

Sunday doesn't seem like Sunday when I don't go to church. I miss it but I'm not able to go. I can easily understand why people get confused on spiritual matters. The more I read the more I'm convinced that everybody is confused about this matter of healing. When I ask questions I get such vague answers. I end up right where I started with the opinion that all I can do is make my requests known to God and leave the results with Him. 11:00 A.M.

12:25 P.M.

I've forgotten what a day without pain feels like. I'm not even allowed the luxury of crying because it hurts to cry. My apologies —once more I've sunk into the trap of feeling sorry for myself.

It's now 1:25 P.M. and would you believe I'm feeling good? Lord, I'm so glad I know You and that You care so much about me.

7:00 P.M.

Mrs. Hanson has been a blessing to my heart during this time of illness. Most people forget you after a week or so. Only two members of the church have kept in contact with me. I'm not complaining; I'm very grateful. I have friends outside the church who have remained faithful and concerned. All of this makes me see myself all too clearly. I'm afraid my Christian life has certainly been nothing to brag about 7:15 P.M.

July 15 3:00 P.M.

In the early hours Pat's son-in-law was shot—the policeman, Erville Brown. He's in critical condition. Lord, please be with the family. As far as I know he's a Christian. Something like this can be more of a strain on the loved ones than on the victim. What about the one who shot him? What's he thinking of? Does he feel remorse? Lord, we need You more than we realize. If I didn't know You, I'd probably kill myself in a hurry, because I'm constantly scared.

There's such a beautiful difference between hope and hopeless. That difference is You, Lord, and once again I find myself praising and thanking You for caring so much. 3:30 P.M.

9:10 P.M.

Pat's son-in-law died. With all my heart I hope he's with You, Lord. My heart goes out to his wife; I cannot imagine the loss she must be feeling now. Lord, please make Your presence known to her in this time of need. Today has been a good day for me physically and I thank You for it, Lord. The preacher came by tonight and as usual it was good to talk with him. Rini called and once more, Lord, You've heard and answered prayers. The whole family will be so pleased to know that Rick will be stationed closer to home.

July 16

Maria Estes has been taking me to the doctor for the last couple of days. I'm more than fortunate when it comes to family and friends. They've sincerely wanted to help. Marilyn is coming in the morning. I look forward to her coming. She's really been fantastic. She's quite a nurse as she anticipates my needs before I have time to voice them. I love Marilyn and feel better just being with her.

Babs and Brackman came over tonight. This was the first time we had met him. Eugene and I both liked him. They plan to get married next month and I wish them both love and happiness. Thank You, Lord, for another good day.

July 17 8:40 A.M.

Lord, today is the first day in I don't know when that I woke up without feeling the least bit bad. Thank You very much.

11:40 P.M.

Lord, the day is almost gone. I still feel good physically and mentally. In January I felt that all this was for a reason—that You had a specific purpose and wanted something from me. I wondered and prayed some about it but didn't go much further with it. Are you trying to tell me something again? Lord, I want to do or be what You want, so help me to know. 12:50 P.M.

July 18

Thirteen years ago I was also involved with doctors and nurses when Betty was born. My life has been filled with events. Naturally they weren't all happy events. Lord, I don't always understand why things happen the way they do and I don't think You always expect me to, but when You do, help me not to be too lazy to try to find out. 10:25 P.M.

July 19 3:55 P.M.

Marilyn met Mrs. Hanson today before she went home. I've

talked a lot to Marilyn about Mrs. Hanson so I was glad for them to meet. Mrs. Hanson brought me a nutritious drink plus food for thought, as always, and things to read. I can't be thankful enough for her. She's cared about me physically and she's cared about me mentally as well as spiritually. What more could I ask? When I'm well and the opportunity arises, dear Lord, I hope and pray that I will do the same for someone in need. 4:10 P.M.

Babs and Brackman came by again tonight. Lord, I'm really fortunate to have a friend like Babs. You know that shortly she'll be going into the hospital. I ask that You'll be as real to her and bless her as You have me. I know she's uneasy for going into the hospital doesn't exactly make a person joyful. This I also know, if she'll put her faith in You, You'll give her courage that will surprise her.

Thanks for the song, "I asked the Lord"—it's been a comfort to me. I didn't know I could laugh, cry and pray all at the same time. I always thought tears of joy were silly until now. It took a lot to open my eyes, didn't it, Lord? If I died within the next minute I could at least say I'd felt some good honest emotions.

July 20 6:45 P.M.

I've had to eat a little every hour today to avoid getting sick, but it worked so I'm not complaining. Eugene put up some corn, tomatoes, okra and bell peppers today. I even helped—how about that? My voice sounds awful but hopefully it will be better soon.

I earnestly pray that this suffering will make a better Christian of me than I ever have been in the past. After all, what will have been accomplished if I'm miraculously healed of cancer and then go back to being just as I was before? To be specific, I was a luke-warm Christian. The reason I'm writing all this down is so that I can go back from time to time and refresh my mind. I want to remember that I suffered dreadfully and that during all of it You were more real to me than ever before. Lord, forbid that I should waste so much time and so many opportunities as I did before. 7:20 P.M.

July 21

Sunday isn't the same when I stay at home and don't go to church. With Your help, Lord, I'll be there next Sunday. I wrote the words to "I asked the Lord" down on a piece of paper to give to Ellen. I felt they would be comforting to her during this time of suffering. It's really a beautiful song.

> I asked the Lord to comfort me
> when things weren't going my way;
> He said to me,"I will comfort you,
> and lift your cares away."

July 22 10:00 A.M.

I just finished the last treatment, hallelujah! There were times when I thought I'd never finish. If You hadn't been there, Lord, I'd never have finished. I'm much more of a coward than I thought I was. Now, Lord, I still need You even though I won't be facing that machine each morning. I had a lovely day, again. Thanks, Lord.

July 23 11:45 A.M.

Dr. Bostwick told me yesterday that I was fortunate not to have had some of the problems that a lot of people have. Again I must say, "Thanks, Lord."

Marilyn's friend's sister sent me some books to read. I was never so considerate of other people. I don't deserve the kind consideration from people I don't even know, not to mention those that love me. Lord, I would like to ask You to bless in a very special way all those who have been kind to me. 12:00

July 24

This time tomorrow I will be meeting Rini and Rick. I'm very excited and anxious and yet I wish Eugene were going with me. Not because I'm afraid of flying but because in the past couple of months Eugene has been at my side almost constantly. I've done quite a bit of leaning on him.

July 25

So many times I've lain on the ground and looked skyward trying to imagine being up there. I've been under, beside, in and above the clouds. Now all I lack is being on the clouds jumping from one to another. I could go into a trance just staring out the window—it's unreal.

July 26

I slept the whole night through for the first time in several weeks. And I wasn't sick when I woke up this morning.

Rini's kids are well behaved and don't bother me in any way. Not many people with small children handle them so well. I still can't get over the flight. I really enjoyed. it.

July 27

I'm wondering if Eugene misses me as much as I do him. I miss being held in his arms from time to time during a day. I connect safety with his arms. Maybe that's silly but it's true. I've enjoyed the visit with Rini and I have no choice but to rest. Rini won't let me do anything. Rick treats me just like he's my brother. I couldn't ask for more unless it was Eugene by my side. 11:30 P.M.

July 29

I was feeling bad last night. I don't know whether it was from the drastic cut in pain tablets or from the depression over the article in the magazine. The article was about a cancer patient and the way he died.

I deserved the depression because I let the devil get the upper hand. Forgive me, Lord. For a while there I did like Peter when he walked on the water. Today was a good day: it's so much better putting my problems in capable hands. 11:15 P.M.

July 30 10:55 P.M.

I met Rini's best friend tonight. I can see why Rini formed the attachment. Frances is very much like Marilyn. They'll both probably be meek, mild, and relatively innocent if they live to be one-hundred. Some people are like that. As for me, I'm neither meek nor mild. Sometimes I feel older than my Mother—I mean mentally, I've felt good all day and only took two pain tablets. 11:10 P.M.

August 2

I flew home last night and only You and I, Lord, know how glad I was to be in Eugene's arms once again. I try not to cling to him but find myself doing it in spite of everything. I do believe I need Your help with the problem. It's such a feeling of helplessness that I automatically reach out. That's one of the things that bothers me—my lack of self-confidence.

August 3 1:00 P.M.

It's dismal outside and the same inside. Unfortunately I haven't discovered a magic way to keep my chin up all the time. Sometimes my faith goes out the window and then I quietly go to pieces. Oh, Lord, what a coward I am.

August 5

Yesterday I went to church for the first time in several weeks. It was really nice to be there but my only disappointment was that Preacher Hays didn't preach.

I felt good yesterday, or as I tell Eugene, I never feel good anymore—just less than bad or better than I have felt. Anyway it was a good day.

Today I went to the hospital for a check-up. The doctor said everything is fine as far as he could tell. I asked the doctor what my chances were. He said, "So-so—there is no way of telling, yet." I hated myself for asking him. I know I was just putting him on the spot asking him something that only You know, Lord. I came home depressed and cried a while. I read that it was good for a person to cry once in a while. I did feel better afterwards.

I talked with Celeste and Marilyn this afternoon. Celeste had cancer last year so she knows how I feel. Marilyn knows because she loves me and has lots of compassion. I feel good too, because my other half is home and I just naturally feel better when he's around. 10:00 P.M.

Thanks, Lord. I cried out, and once more You were there. I don't know what I'd do without You. That's all the more reason to tell the lost. What does a lost person do in my situation? I've gone through such agonies I can't even put them down on paper. I had You, Lord, and they have nothing. To think I often feel sorry for myself.

August 6 10:10 P.M.

I did more house work today than I've done in ages. When evening came I was quite tired and had to lie down. I was rather proud of myself but it did make me realize how tired and weak I am.

Tonight Babs and Brackman were married. I love Babs and naturally want her to have all the happiness and love that heaven allows. We like Brackman better each time we're around him. The best thing I could wish for Babs and Brackman is that their love grows and matures through the years. Eugene and I have our squabbles but I wouldn't trade his love for anything. If they look to You, Lord, I'm sure things will be better for them, as they have been for Eugene and me. 10:30 P.M.

August 7 6:45 P.M.

Each day, Lord, I regain a little more strength but it's a slow process. It's not half as slow as the surgery would have been. Lord, help-me not to be impatient. 6:50 P.M.

August 8 7:35 P.M.

Today I stayed at home and took it easy. Mrs. Hanson came over this morning. She's a kind and thoughtful person. I've been in better spirits for the last few days. Lord, you know all I have to do is glance down and before I know it, I'm in despair. That makes me all the happier when I remember to look up.

August 9 9:15 P.M.

Marilyn spent the day with me and insisted that she do some

cleaning while here. Marilyn, Mother and Rini insist on doing for me—that is love. I'm not complaining about their concern because I'd be hurt if they acted as if nothing was wrong.

I had to go to the dentist to have my teeth cleaned. Lord, You heard my prayer and answered it, and I'm so thankful. I felt uneasy and then I prayed. The dentist told me there were no problems on the cancer side of my mouth. I only had two cavities. How wonderful to see prayers answered. Lord, I have so very much to be thankful for.

August 10 9:15 P.M.

Today I did a little yard work. Lord, just a week ago I couldn't have done it. My voice is almost normal for the first time in several weeks. I can now eat almost anything if I chew the food quite a bit.

Your Word, Lord, has given me the peace that I so desperately needed. How can I praise You enough? Lord, help me to make a tremendous effort to be even a little worthy of such loving care. 9:35 P.M.

August 12 12:30 P.M.

I talked with Amy Van Ham, the teacher I probably will work with in kindergarten. School starts week after next and I plan to work unless You direct me otherwise. Amy asked me if I planned to work the whole year.

Lord, how do I answer questions like that? I told her I would be as far as I knew. In a way she was asking if I would be alive. I believe I will be because I'm praying to that end and the Bible teaches that praying by faith can move mountains. Lord, whatever the future I know You'll be right beside me. 12:45 P.M.

August 14 2:45 P.M.

A toothache bothered me last night. Unfortunately I was feeling kind of down yesterday. I try, Lord, but evidently not hard enough. Sometimes I try to carry the load and I just can't. Sometimes I want to commit suicide before the end of the day.

When I have strength it comes from You, Lord. Otherwise I'm down and out. 2:55 P.M.

August 15 6:00 P.M.

Again today I've been in the clutches of gloom. The pathology report from the doctor's office didn't cheer me up either. I don't know why they sent it to me—perhaps they thought I'd like to frame it. Lord, how much can I stand?

I talked with Babs this evening. I don't know whether she realized it or not but she cheered me very much. I value her friendship and hope it will be a lasting one. I think I need to learn to remain emotionally detached, otherwise I'll crack up. For some reason I find it easier to be that way with her than with a lot of people. She doesn't treat me any differently. Thank the Lord for loved ones. 6:30 P.M.

8:00 P.M.

Betty has practically grown up overnight. This evening I looked at her and found myself looking into a face more like an adult's than a child's. She's already passed her Nanny, Aunt Marilyn, Aunt Rini, Aunt Jane in height. She's almost caught up with me in weight. For a while there I wondered, but now I do believe she's going to make a very attractive young lady.

James isn't making any big changes right now. He is getting taller, but he looks pretty much the same as he did two years ago. 8:20 P.M.

August 18 10:45 P.M.

I've been rather busy since Rini and Rick came back so I haven't had a chance to write. I know without doubt that I'm better off busy. Too much extra time leaves me brooding time and that's bad news.

I didn't feel up to going to church today. Strangely enough I feel better tonight than I've felt all day. I usually feel worse toward night. My feelings are totally unpredictable, even to me.

I'm worried about Mom and Dad. I don't understand what's

happening. Daddy talks about faith but doesn't exercise it. Lord, when it comes down to the nitty-gritty, do most people toss their faith aside and try to work things out without Your help? I guess I'm guilty of that too. At this time I may not be so quick to try to work it out myself because I know I can't do anything at all without your help except go stark, raving crazy. Lord, why do we have such independent natures?

August 22 6:55 P.M.

Yesterday I went to school for teachers' workday. Everything went smoothly. I believe I can enjoy working as a teachers' aid with Amy—at least I feel comfortable with her. Rini and Rick left yesterday to get settled in Jacksonville. I don't feel I had much of a summer except for the time I went to Louisiana. And then I had to avoid getting in the sun.

I have no idea how or if I'll be able to continue working but I'm sure going to try. I believe it would be detrimental to my mental health to allow myself too much free time. I suppose I'm a selfish person because inevitably when I have spare time my thoughts turn inward.

I noticed that some people at school accepted me back happily and sincerely. I must point out that the very girl who has mentioned religious matters and talked the most about a personal knowledge of You, Lord, is more uneasy around me than others. Why? Is it because all that talk was just talk? She looks at me as if I had three heads. Some people probably subconsciously think they might catch cancer or perhaps the thoughts of it depress them to the point where they would rather avoid me. That's okay because they'd probably depress me, too. Thanks for a happy day, Lord. 10:10 P.M.

August 23 7:15 P.M.

Thanks, Lord, for another happy day. It's amazing how content one can be just living each moment. I find that I can take things in stride or with situations better that way. For a while I felt on the verge of tears frequently. Either I've overcome the problem or maybe I don't have the reasons that I had. It's much simpler for me to let You do the worrying—after all, Lord, You are better equipped to handle my problems.

I spent the morning cleaning the laundry room and game room. That was quite a job, probably the most physical work that I've done at one time since before the biopsy. I enjoyed being able to work. 7:45 P.M.

August 24

I've been concerned about Eugene lately. He's been pushing himself pretty hard. Time spent at home finds him totally exhausted. His conversation seems to center on the jobs or material things. I don't know how to handle this. Maybe my situation depresses him and if it does I suppose I should make some changes. Maybe I should keep my thoughts and feelings to myself.

Lord, You've given me more peace than I thought possible: I'd like to request some of the same for Eugene. In finding peace for myself I overlooked the possibility that he might not have found the same thing.

Then on the other hand there's the possibility that he doesn't think about my situation anywhere near as much as I do. Maybe he's completely trusting when I have a tendency to stumble along, up sometimes and down at other times. At any rate, please help me not to be wrapped up in me. I don't want to be selfish. 12:30 P.M.

6:07 P.M.

Eugene called me to tell me he would be late. Is it my imagination or is it for real? He sounds more at ease on the phone than he does when he's here.

10:25 P.M.

Eugene's home: once again I feel complete.

August 25 9:55 P.M.

Betty and I went to church this morning while Eugene stayed

home with James. Marilyn and family came over and what started as a nice day ended with me in a mental uproar. Eugene and Jack wanted to take off and go to Florida for a few days. I objected and I think I became a target for Jack's bad feelings. I don't know whether it was because he's been uptight over his jobs or because he was mad because I didn't want Eugene to leave me and go to Florida. It wasn't the first time that I've felt like a target for Jack's arrows. I don't know whether he puts me on the defensive or if I do him.

Lord, there are some days that I'd be better off if I stayed in bed and I believe this was one of them. Lord, if I said anything offensive to You, You know I'm sorry but I don't know how else you can learn some things without asking questions. I believe I'd be better off keeping my mouth shut than to open it and be attacked.
I went back to church tonight and to reiterate what I told Pat H. the other day, I love my church and what it stands for. It feels so wonderful to be in the Lord's house. 10:30 P.M.

August 26 9:05 P.M.

I went back to work today and things went better than I expected—I wasn't nearly as tired as I thought I'd be. I feel much more relaxed with Amy than I did last year with Melross. I hope I'll become close to Amy. I feel somewhat alone with Babs gone. She was the only one at school who meant a lot to me. Maybe that's an example of being lonely in a crowd.

I still feel very much apart from most people. I'm with people often but rarely a part of the group. I hear conversations but nine times out of ten they are meaningless.

I never realized how much people think in terms of the future. After the past year, talk of future automatically separates me. Don't think I'm being negative and not trusting the Lord for what He says He'll do—I know He will. It's just that a basic truth has been brought home to me—simply this: right now is what's important in my life, not yesterday or tomorrow. When it comes down to it I can only deal with the situation that I'm involved in at the moment. I don't even know if there'll be a tomorrow, so why should I waste a lot of time making plans for something that might not exist? When it comes down to it, no one does—most people do a lot of assuming. I do have a future but not the one that's most commonly talked about. Once again, Lord, thank You for making a future possible for such as me. 10:10 P.M.

August 27 10:40 P.M.
I had another fine day. I'm sure I'm better off working but I don't want to neglect anything more important. There are lots of things more important than working—for example, Eugene, the kids, and maybe housework. I can't work at school and do loads of work at home, too. I know I'm not physically up to all that. Lord, help me not to overdo things and yet help me not to take advantage of my illness. Help me to be honest with You first, Lord, then me, then Eugene and then the world. My moments are so often beautiful. Lord, thank You for each one. 11:00 P.M.

August 28 9:25 P.M.
Another fine day—granted I'm tired by nightfall; but who isn't? I'm still having trouble with that tooth but the dentist says nothing is wrong. I don't understand it. Tomorrow at school I'm curious to see how the whole groups of children will react to one another. We'll have full classes tomorrow, and then I'll know how well I'll be able to hold up. It's in the 90's so I feel wilted before the day gets going. 9:45 P.M.

August 29 9:15 P.M.
School went fine today and the large groups went much better than I expected. At lunch time today I had difficulties swallowing. I got choked and ended up giving up my lunch. My throat only hurts when I eat and try to swallow.

Rini called last night—it seems they are moving back to Alexandria, Louisiana. I can't imagine Eugene living in one state and me in another and visiting once a month. I suspect their marriage is in trouble. Lord, they're going to need You. 9:45 P.M.

51

August 31 12:05 P.M.

I went to the hospital yesterday and my neck and mouth were thoroughly checked. Doctors Williams and Bostwick said that everything was fine as far as they could tell. Dr. Bostwick always makes me feel good—he's optimistic. I thank the Lord for people who don't look on the gloomy side of everything. He and I both know that he can't promise that the cancer won't start again but then too, he doesn't know that it will, so why be gloomy about it?

I'm very fortunate in the people I've been in contact with during all of this. Just a few lemons. I see God's hand in so many things. It's really true His grace is sufficient for me. Every time I've reached the place where I felt I couldn't possibly go any further, He took over and made it possible. Then, too, He saw to it that I was cheered in countless ways. 12:25 P.M.

September 2 7:00 P.M.

Tomorrow starts another work week. Lord, I need You.

September 3 11:15 P.M.

We listened to Eugene's Bob Harrington tape while Babs and Brackman were here. It thrills me to see Babs so happy.

I haven't felt too super today. Some days I'm just plagued while Satan waits for me to look away from my Saviour. It's odd but I've underestimated both Satan and Jesus for years.

September 4 8:12 P.M.

Lord, You know I've had to push myself today to stay on my feet. I don't know what's wrong but I sure have ached. I woke up about 4:30 A.M. feeling terrible. I took a pain tablet so I could go to work. Lord, You know how terrified I get when I start having problems. I know Your promises about watching over me—it's just that it's so hard to remember them when my body feels so battered and worn.

I'm beginning to have quite a problem trying to keep from getting bitter about the situation. I'm sorry, Lord, but if I could die quickly it would be a relief. Forgive me if I'm being unpleasing to you.

September 5 8:00 P.M.

The doctor said my throat was infected and gave me penicillin. Maybe that's why my throat's been so sore and accounts for all the aching.

I've been watching a special on Evel Knievel—I wonder about such a careless attitude towards life. It appears that no matter, people seem to live their times in the sun and then life on earth is over. Then eternity is according to their acceptance or rejection of You, Lord. 9:20 P.M.

September 7 11:08 P.M.

Another day fades into night and I must say I've felt much better. The thanks goes to drugs or I call it "artificial feel good." I called Dr. Bostwick and he called in some pain medicine to tide me over this weekend. When I'm able to take the pain without becoming all unglued and rebellious then I'll know that I'm letting the Lord take His rightful place in my life. Lord, please forgive me for being so impatient.

We went to see Babs and Brackman tonight. Babs plans to start back to work next week, Lord. You know she'll really need You. Like me she's spent a lot of the summer sick in bed. Help her.

September 8 7:25 P.M.

I planned to go to church but I got strangled on a penicillin capsule. After that I gave up on the idea.

8:00 P.M.

Marilyn called to check on me. I told Eugene about her offering to get the kids for the weekend so I could rest. Eugene and I agree that few people are as fortunate as I am when it comes to loved ones. Marilyn and Mom have gone out of their way to help me many, many times. Others have helped too, but not as often or as much as Mom and Marilyn.

Back to the hospital tomorrow. Lord, help me not to feel so scared. That business about dying a thousand deaths is sheer baloney. Since January I've bit the dust at the very least two or three million times. The only part that fits me is coward. I've daydreamed about dying a painless death many times. Paul in Philippians 1:20 talked about glorifying God with his body, whether in life or death. I admire Paul but I'm afraid I don't measure up in any way to Paul, much less to Christ. Unfortunately, I'm mostly inclined to want the easiest and least painful situations for me. That may be ugly but I'm telling it like it is. 8:30 P.M.

September 9 10:15 P.M.

Dr. Bostwick said my throat was a little red—probably a virus—but he couldn't find anything wrong. At any rate I went back to work. When I feel I need to get off, that's what I'll do, because I'm more important than the job. I felt more relaxed and content today than I have for a week, not to mention just plain feeling a whole lot better physically. For days like this I'm truly thankful.

September 10 10:15 P.M.

I walked up to see Ailene tonight after supper. Ailene's husband asked me if I was all right now. I wonder about people that ask that question—and people from varied backgrounds and different amounts of education have asked. Are they naive or ignorant? They do it without hesitation. I must look like the type that can take anything. I'm proud of myself though, 'cause when he asked I said "I hope so," and let it pass.

September 11 10:05 P.M.

Lord, I'm so grateful for this good day. I'm so much better I can hardly believe it. No doubt about it, my faith still needs improvement. Lord, help me to understand Your Word. Help me not to waste my time on things You'd rather I left alone. If I could form the habit of having You on my mind almost all the time I'm sure I could do better.

September 12 :10:25 P.M.

I don't want to give in to the illness one bit because if I do I'm lost. It's so easy to become tangled in self-pity. Without even realizing it I can suddenly switch from a good mood to depression. Sometimes I know why I get depressed and sometimes I don't have any idea.

September 14 9:20 P.M.

It's really one super adjustment, living with the knowledge that you've had cancer. Will it always hover over me? It is never far from me. I don't want to dwell on the possibilities of what the cancer will or won't do but sometimes it's as if I'm hypnotized and can't stop myself. It's a vicious merry-go-round. One day I'm up, the next I'm down.

Eugene and Jack went to Florida to go deep-sea fishing. I'm always somewhat down when Eugene is away. Perhaps I'm too dependent.

September 15 10:00 P.M.

We went to church this morning and again tonight. I love going to church. I can't imagine not being free to go whenever I want to and yet I know that's true in some places. Lord, how often I take privileges for granted. Preacher Hays talked about being in the will of God and knowing it. Maybe I'm dense, Lord, but I can't say that I know I'm doing just as You'd have me do. I want to but I don't understand how I know for sure.

September 16 10:08 P.M.

Today has been busy but happy. First there was school, then the dentist and eye doctor. The tooth problem was less serious than I had thought. I wasn't too pleased to find that James is near-sighted, but I should be grateful that we can afford to get glasses for him.

I turned off "Medical Center" when I discovered it was about a lady with cancer trying to decide whether to rely on God or the doctor.

I made that decision some time back. Preacher Hays in his own special way pointed out that God gives knowledge to doctors, so why not accept what they can do while knowing full well that the final outcome is where it's always been. I have doctors that can do wonders and God who can do anything. Thank You, Lord, for Your peace and love. Your presence is so precious.

I've spilled many tears this year in pity for me, some because of physical pain, and many because I felt Your love and nearness so strongly.

I had a lovely surprise waiting for me. Eugene was here. I stepped in the back door and was quietly folded into the most lovely arms in all the world. Next I heard beautiful words, "Did you miss me? I love you, and I missed you." Now I ask you, could I ask for more?

September 16 10:40 P.M.

I must remember to let others know I care because it is a very warm and fulfilling way to feel. We need to express our love by letting others know that we care. What's wrong with saying, "I care if you're unhappy," "I care if you don't feel well," or "I care if you're happy." What's wrong with spilling over with love towards others?

September 17 10:15 P.M.

I've moved up a little, education and status wise and yet it's meaningless. At one time it would have meant a lot but now I could turn my back to it all. I think how much I wanted that diploma, how tickled I was to get the job and how I felt Clayton Junior College was pretty special. But now, all I think is "You silly fool." I never guessed that it would all become so blah. I feel indifferent. I couldn't care less about the job. So what do I do now? I don't want to waste any of my time.

September 19 10:15 P.M.

Maybe I'm wrong but I don't believe Amy is quite at ease with me. She mentioned praying once but I understand that doesn't mean she's a Christian. She hasn't really said or done anything to make me think she was. Lord, I sure need Your help. If the opportunity arises help me not to miss it.

Mrs. Hanson came by tonight and I enjoyed talking with her. She has been faithful as few Christians ever are, myself included.

She and my family and certainly Preacher Hays have all been faithful. I dare say the day he took me for treatment did me as much good as the treatment. Things he said still pop into my mind. The song, "I asked the Lord to comfort me," says at the end of it, "I thank the Lord for everything," and I, like the writer of the song, am also very thankful. My Saviour's love surrounds me so many times, that I feel overwhelmed. I know I'm loved and cared for in a mighty way.

September 20 9:00 P.M.

It's strange the way I jump from one mood to another without any apparent reason. It leaves me stunned. If it surprises me then how do loved ones cope with me? I keep it pretty much under control with outsiders but it's too much to carry all the time. With loved ones I'm forced to act as I feel to a great extent. I let my hair down quite a bit in this diary but almost always I hold back a certain amount. That leaves some things that words can't express —only You know, Lord. Many times I've wanted to express my feelings but they were too brutal sounding for the average person to understand.

Disease is something people prefer to dismiss—so would I but I didn't get a choice. Perhaps I don't have the disease now but learning to cope with its mental strain is by no means a laughing matter.

Sometimes I'm unable to make myself get out of the depression, but most of the time one of these usually works—a crying spell (alone), music to drown my thoughts, then last but certainly not least I turn to my Saviour and when I trust and believe Him, well, He gives me joy and peace beyond anything I've ever experienced prior to the illness.

I know that a person is in the process of dying from the day he's born, but until my twenty-ninth year I never really thought of it as a part of my life. More and more I'm able to take the moment for whatever it's worth. Some moments are so full of joy and love that I'm thrilled. 9:35 P.M.

September 21 9:50 P.M.

I can't make up my mind whether I want to quit reading and

watching programs concerning cancer. Sometimes they leave me quite depressed, but at other times, hopeful. I guess I'll probably keep right on because I'm the type that wants to know everything —good, bad or indifferent.

Upon occasion I am a glutton for punishment, because some things I read don't sound too encouraging. But I'll overcome. I've always been a fighter, not a quitter. When there's nothing to struggle for, then it will be the time to quit. Life is precious but I'm not sure how precious or to what extent one should struggle to stay a part of life on earth. I don't mean to sound down because I feel good and happy today. It's just that I'm very curious about the way I feel.

September 22 4:50 P.M.

It's strange to me that I usually get so strung out on Sunday evenings that I could scream. I know all about a day of rest but my family just plain isn't restful. I actually rest better when I'm alone, and that's rare. I enjoy having a little time to read and to put down my thoughts, but I have to squeeze in those things. Eugene, Betty, and James—especially Eugene and James—can spend hours in front of the television, but it drives me up the wall.

I enjoy church but not the rest of the day. I feel I must be dreadfully lacking in something. I keep thinking I should give up my job but I hesitate to do so. It's not that I don't feel able to do it but I'm just not satisfied. Lord, I really need Your help. 5:23 P.M.

September 23 8:47 P.M.

My bald spot is going away. When the hair fell out during the treatments I was convinced that it wouldn't grow back. I was delighted the other night to discover that it was no longer bare. I know that sounds vain, but that's typical of me.

9:55 P.M.

I read my daily Bible reading just now and, strangely enough, it promoted doing what you can with what you have. Maybe I try to make something difficult out of simple things.

September 24 8:47 P.M.

I came home in a somewhat bad mood, once again for no

reason, just felt somewhat down. If I have a few aches it automatically throws me into a tailspin. I told Eugene I had one of my suicide days—one in which I dream up painless ways to die. Cowardly, perhaps, but one who hasn't been in this predicament shouldn't judge. I know I could be in worse shape physically but sometimes it's more than I can handle mentally.

When I'm like this Eugene is so comforting and understanding it makes me feel unworthy. He carries quite a load himself. Lord, forgive me for not completely trusting.

9:10 P.M.

I just talked with Mrs. Hanson about doing something to fill this void. She suggested some visitation on Saturday evening. I must remember not to get so wrapped up in me that I can't see beyond.

September 25 10:00 P.M.

Betty and I went to church tonight and I for one was very glad I did. We're learning how to do successful soul-winning. Different people have been acting out visitation situations. It's very enlightening. After church I talked with Preacher Hays and, as always, I felt much better afterwards. He helps simplify so many things, and, Lord, You know I'm thankful for people I can talk with openly. We've never had a preacher like him and I guess there's never been a time that I've needed someone like him as much.

Lord, I see You in so much. I'm really ashamed when I let things and situations get me down. I want to be able to do at least a few things in my life that will be pleasing to You.

A little boy said something today that was truly beautiful. He said, "The devil will get you for being bad." I asked him, "What do you do about it?" And he said, "I say, 'Forgive me.'" So simple and sweet, Lord, straight from a child. Lord, help me to be simple and direct.

September 26 8:00 P.M.

I've felt peaceful and more content today than I have for some time. I'm glad I talked with Preacher Hays last night. I wonder if

I'll ever come near overcoming the problem of being wrapped up in me. At least when I talk with him, I'm able to look at the situation more sensibly. I've tried to put my finger on just why I feel better after talking with him and I can only conclude that he's a Christian, he cares, and yet he's not personally involved. I suppose that's why I can talk easily with him and say what I feel without shocking him or making him feel torn apart.

Lots of times I want to strike out or lash out at something or someone just to release some of my frustrations. Sometimes it's beyond me to remember that others have been and are in worse shape. All I can do is cry, "Why, why, why?" As the little boy told me yesterday, I can only say, "Forgive me."

September 27 9:00 P.M.

It's ironic that I look forward to weekends because I'm rushed all week, and yet if I weren't busy I'd probably go all to pieces. Maybe I look inward too much as the book says—the one that Preacher Hays loaned me.

I don't quite know how I can quit thinking about the past and look to the future, when the past is more comfortable to look at than the future. I'm not sure which way to look. Mostly I'm afraid to look to the future and the past hasn't offered a whole lot of comfort. Oh, well, there's now.

Believe it or not I'm not depressed. I guess I've made more adjustments than even I realized.

September 29 2:25 P.M.

I'm enjoying a little time alone this Sunday. I feel the ever pressing urge to cram in as much as I can. Is that common among people who have had cancer? There's an urgency in everything I do. As each month comes to an end I wonder if it's my last. If so, what have I accomplished?

I enjoy Mrs. Hanson as a teacher and a person. It was quite an experience yesterday for me to go on visitation with her. In Sunday School she mentioned that women should watch their relationships with their pastor. I guess I should watch myself as I tend to go overboard with everything. I already think of him as way beyond the average male. In all honesty some people are beyond average.

September 30 9:00 P.M.

Today hasn't been super great but not super bad either. I'm still having that weird twitch when I bend my head down. It's almost like a shock. I don't know if it has something to do with my neck or my nerves.

One good thing, I feel better about my job since I talked with Preacher Hays. At least I don't feel like I'm wasting time. I have so much to be thankful for. My beautiful moments are quite numerous. Maybe I notice them more now.

October 1 9:05 P.M.

I felt fine until I started having trouble swallowing tonight. For a while I lost control of things. I went to the doctor about my ear, and he gave me ear drops and told me to come back if I still had trouble.

O, Lord, am I falling apart? Have You forgotten me? I know things could be worse but that's getting hard to remember.

October 2 9:30 P.M.

The skits on visitation and soul-winning at church are very informing. There's a lot for me to learn.

Today was better than yesterday, but I can't pull out of those down moods as fast as I'd like to. I'm filled with "I wonder ifs," and "maybes" when I look to myself instead of to God. By myself I can't do anything, least of all stay sane. All this trouble started a year ago this month. The first miracle is that I'm reasonably sane most of the time. From there on, I've had quite a few miracles.

October 4 9:35 P.M.

Probably my biggest mistake is underestimating the devil and his co-workers. He and they really do wonders with me if I don't keep my eyes toward God, then they'll be able to ruin any testimony I might have. Amy has been asking in a roundabout way what I believe. I feel it's very important to give the right answers.

October 7

Rini and Rick came in Wednesday night. What can I say about those two except if they're sane I must be stark-raving crazy.
They're moving back to Georgia!

My ear is driving me wild so I've been on edge. I have an appointment with a specialist. I don't think I'm going to spend a fortune in doctor's offices. Maybe it would be better to let it ride until I can't stand it anymore and then take action. I often feel like I should totally put myself in the hands of the Lord and back completely away from doctors. So far I don't have much faith in them.

Lord, it's been a year since this nightmare started and even now it seems unreal. The life that I thought was so precious no longer is. I've lost count of the times I've been tempted to end it all, not to mention the times I've looked hopefully skyward hoping to see the Saviour coming. I try not to live in fear because that's not trusting, but a certain amount seems to be ever present. It hovers over me to make itself known when I'm fortunate enough to forget for a little while. The torment of fearing pain is something to cope with like I never even imagined. Why can't I completely trust? Is it the human part of me or am I trying to blame Satan for something that's my own fault?
11:05 P.M.

October 12

It's really wonderful to have a painless day—lovely. A day without physical or mental pain is a joy I don't often have. It probably takes pain to make me appreciate not having any. To experience complete peace for short periods must be similar to heaven.

When stark reality becomes too much then I slip into a dream-like state that locks out the unpleasant. I'm not always able to do this, and when I can't it is quite a strain on me.

Lord, I'm so grateful for all You've done for me. You know I'm somewhat of a dreamer and if I weren't I couldn't take all this. I'm so glad to have Someone know and completely understand how I feel, especially Someone who can do something about it.

October 13
Preacher Hays brought out a couple of things in his sermon that I had thought about. One was this thing about being afraid. Only a little better than a year ago I wouldn't have known what he was talking about. The other was about taking your own life. I understood what he was saying and I appreciated the way he said it.

When I need to talk I'm glad I have someone who's realistic. I can do without empty meaningless phrases such as "Hang in there!" Hanging in there is fine except I need to know how. Another cute one is "Don't let it get you down." I might ask, "Down to what?" Six foot under, probably. 10:15 P.M.

October 14
Eugene took James to the doctor and kept him home today because he has a bad cold. This evening the ear specialist said I have a partial loss of hearing in my left ear due to some antibiotics that I took during my illness. I found out that I wasn't imagining the noise. After the hearing test the specialist suggested that when the noise bothered me to drown it out with another noise. Forty minutes of his time, an educated guess, and the bit about drowning out the noise cost $35.

Do doctors lessen people's suffering or prolong their misery? When they supposedly prolong your life do they really do you a favor? How precious is life?

Each day Eugene is dearer to me and I'm fully aware that I don't deserve him, but nevertheless I'm glad he's a part of my life. We're an odd combination and I often try to figure us out. It can only be You, Lord, who binds us together because we're as opposite as can be. I'm never completely at ease when I'm away from him. Is it always that way with married couples? The clinging is probably due to my illness, but I was somewhat like that before I knew about the cancer. Eugene is a special type person.

I hated to jump Betty last night but she has been getting slack

63

about a lot of things. She's too smart to make poor grades. I wonder if I'm failing somewhere. I realize that she's done much better in the past. I don't want to be so wrapped up in me that I fail her and James. If they need help, Lord, help me to see it.

October 15

I must admit that at times I'm deliberately blunt. I'm not sure why I do or say things like I do. Maybe it's an outlet for frustrations or a way of getting back at someone. I know I'm pretty blunt with Eugene but not to get at him. I think with him it's a matter of having to say what I feel rather than bottle it up. So often I bottle it up with other people that I think if I had to do the same with Eugene I'd crack under the pressure.

Eugene put James on his back and carried him to bed. It was as if James were four years old again. It took me back a few years when I saw them galloping up the hall. The hall rang with James' laughter. Lord, so many moments are precious. For example, as Betty was leaving to go to Sarah's, Eugene called out to her, "Don't let Clifton get you." Her reply was, "Oh, Daddy." Probably a year ago I wouldn't have noticed such things. It's amazing how little things become precious.

October 20

As usual I blinked and my weekend was gone. Marilyn and family spent Friday night and Saturday with us. I rested today as my throat and neck have bothered me. Lord, only You know how much I'd like to quickly die. I push myself continuously to keep going and sometimes I get so tired of pushing that I desperately want to end it all.

I want to be cheerful and uncomplaining but, oh, God, You know how I struggle. I want to avoid being bitter but that too is beginning to be a problem. I'm just not one of those sweet and lovely type Christians.

Preacher Hays emphasized that Paul was in tears frequently. I wonder why I've always struggled so hard not to cry. Now I can't control the tears. Some tears come because of the physical pain and some roll down my cheeks because the mental strain becomes more than I can bear. Sleep keeps me going at times. I'm thankful that I sleep well.

October 21

My daily Bible reading fit today perfectly. It talked about how when one thing goes wrong, other things also go to pieces rapidly. That's the way my day started and it got worse before it ended.

October 22

Today is Marilyn's 32nd birthday. It seems only yesterday that she and I were walking to school on icy cold mornings with our arms loaded with school books. Although I'm 30 I feel 80 and that's not exaggerating.

I am forever looking for places and times to be alone. I don't have many moments to quietly reflect over the day. I feel tired so much that I want to get to bed as soon as possible. I still have the odd twinge in my legs and lower back when I bend my head down. The noise in my left ear almost sounds like a pulse. My lips stay parched from dryness.

People are extremely curious about my reaction to having cancer, so inevitably the conversations get around to me and my feelings. It's impossible for me to dismiss the subject even for a short while. Maybe I wasn't meant to. Frequently it hurts—the way people can be so insensitive about it, but even that has begun to be dulled. After a while maybe I won't feel it at all.

I'm beginning to enjoy the book Preacher Hays loaned me. Quite a bit of what the author says about spiritual depression fits me to a tee. There's a lot that doesn't apply but he's come closer to my specific problems than a lot of other books.

October 25

Today was a fine day. I've felt more at peace with myself lately. It's so easy to start looking down but the damage it causes is devastating. My miseries are multiplied a million times from simply trying to depend on myself or just looking downward instead of heavenward.

This thing of fear has really been a battle and it's only in the last few days that I've realized that it too has to be turned over to the Lord. The book that Preacher Hays loaned me has been a great deal of help.

October 29

My neck has hurt almost all day on the left side, so naturally I'm frazzled. We took Betty to a football game tonight, but Eugene and I came home before the game was over. Betty stayed with Sarah. The benches were hard, I was tired, and Eugene was bored. I'm not depressed but if the Lord offered me a quick and easy death I'd gladly accept. 9:55 P.M.

October 30

My neck didn't bother me today so I felt much happier. When I'm relaxed I feel so much better mentally and physically. Betty and I went to church tonight and I talked at length with Preacher Hays after church. Only the Lord knows how much it helps for me to be able to talk with him.

So many times I get bogged down something fierce, and when I do it's not always good to burden the family. They love me but when I make negative remarks it hurts them and yet I need to be able to say exactly what I feel. Sometimes I just can't take the old "everything's gonna be fine" bit, especially from people who are fine as far as they know. I want to scream "Who are you to tell me how I should feel?"

November 2

Time is ticking by and I find myself surprised to be alive. Five months ago I didn't expect to be still among the living. I don't know any more now than I did then except that one can eventually adjust to uncertainty. Each day of my life has become special. I know there's a special reason for the last few months. I'm fulfilling a special purpose, so that must be good. I had some time to be alone today and I needed that. It was nice. 11:25 P.M.

November 5

Today my Bible reading was about waiting on God. How much time in my life has been spent in waiting? Waiting for buses, waiting in lines at stores, at the court house to pay taxes, waiting in doctor's offices, dental offices, waiting to see someone, waiting, waiting, waiting, waiting to live, and finally waiting to die.

Why do I have problems waiting on the Lord? Maybe I'll eventually learn. I know this past year has taught me quite a bit about waiting and yet I have a lot to learn.

November 6

Tonight at church Preacher Hays said that sometimes you have to put yourself in God's hands. Well, I am already there.

I feel like I'm living in limbo. It's hard to live with certain uncertainties. That sounds crazy but that's the way it is.

November 7

I've felt on the verge of tears all evening. I might even say I've felt on the verge of hysterics. Mom and Dad came this evening but I couldn't pull myself out of the mood. Poor Mom and Dad.

November 8

Marilyn, Rini, Betty and I went shopping tonight. I finished more Christmas shopping so I'm very tired but that's the way I want it. Idle time leads to thoughts I can't cope with.

November 9

Christmas shopping wears me out, staying on the go so much. I'm just beat and the roaring noise in my ear is bothering me again. Long conversations are out of the question, because my throat, mouth and lips get so dry that it's very painful to talk. If the conversation is trivial I find it next to impossible to keep listening. I don't mean to be rude but find myself getting so strung out I want to scream or pound the walls with my fists.

November 12

I've been strung out for the last few days. I usually get that way when I have to go to the hospital for my check-ups. For some stupid reason I try to prepare myself for whatever might be found, and naturally, in preparing myself I think of the worst possible things. Both doctors said everything was fine as far as they could tell. I was pleased that they didn't find anything.

I felt happy as a lark and sad too as I left. Sad because there is so much terrible sickness—I have seen so much pain and misery there, that even when I get good news it's hard to rejoice. I realize all too well that I could get to be like one of those I see. Does it upset me because I'm close to it or because they're people and while they're living they feel pain the same as I do? Do you only learn to feel genuine concern when you've been in the same situation? I look back and wonder if I ever cared before.

With all my heart, Lord, I wish we could have done like You planned. Lord, help me never to stop caring, loving, and feeling, even if it's painful. I've spent a lot of time caring mostly about me.

November 14

Heaven has got to be one super special place. Being minus physical pain will make it super special but being minus mental pains and struggling will make it beyond words.

I can almost hear Jack Holcomb singing:

> After the toil and the heat of the day,
> After my troubles are past,
> After the sorrows are taken away,
> I shall see Jesus at last.

November 17

My lovely weekend is almost gone—it's Sunday night and I'm listening to the lonely sound of rain hitting the house. I know rain is imperative but for some reason I always feel lonely when it rains and sometimes it makes me feel down.

We had a wonderful service in church this morning. Howard Morris, a retired minister, preached. He blessed the hearts of many with his sermon, obviously heaven sent. You can tell he's sitting on the ready. He's in his seventies but he has a very refreshing way of preaching. He preaches a simple, direct message in a mighty way. I'm so thankful for brothers and sisters in Christ, for they've meant so much so many times—especially this past year.

November 25

Once again I feel as if I'm killing time, and that I find almost unbearable. Since January '74 I can't stand the thought of not using all of my time in a useful way. That wasn't meant to sound pious or smug. I know me well enough to know I've still got a lot of room for improvement. I feel I need to cram in a lot because I've wasted a lot of time. Maybe I'm pushing too hard. That may be why I feel so strung out much of the time.

There again, it's a matter of deciding whether to keep pushing or relax and be idle. The latter is impossible because I relax only when I sleep. If my body gets too idle then my mind is far from idle. When my mind is preoccupied with others I'm fairly safe but when it turns inward the destructive forces take their toll.

I told Eugene I find it odd that nearly all the things I've read recently, and that's a lot, get around to this business of the mind passing disease to the body. I wonder if these books are telling me something? I can't come up with any outstanding events prior to January '74. If there are any I've done a super job of repressing them.

I've been listening to the tapes, "God's Woman," which Mrs. Hanson brought. I'm astounded—I didn't realize that I'm so icky about submitting to my husband. I don't want to have a rebellious spirit but I'm afraid I do.

After this past year I should be meek and submissive. I admire people that are mild-mannered and gentle, but, Lord, I don't fit any of those nice adjectives. I don't picture me saying to Eugene, "Yes, dear—whatever you say, dear." I can only react—yuk —and pray for whatever it is that I need.

November 26

Amy surprises me in lots of ways. About the time I feel like throwing my hands in the air and giving up, I catch a glimpse of a different Amy. I think she keeps another personality hidden

69

that I would actually prefer. I know it's not unusual to hide parts of ourselves from others but I'd think most people would hide the rotten parts rather than the good. Maybe I'll get to know the other Amy V. before the school year is over.

We've spent a great deal of time at school this week talking about Thanksgiving. While I'm thinking about Thanksgiving I might note that I have quite a bit to be thankful for right about now. I'm surprised to be alive not to mention living without being in a lot of pain. In February of last year I wrote that I had a personal Saviour who is interested in my welfare. I rejoice in saying He still is.

November 27

I'm convinced that the church doesn't come anywhere near meeting the needs of the average person. I ask myself, why do I go? What's the point in the assembly? What really happens at the altar? Maybe I'm seriously lacking but I look about me at the services and something is missing. I understand the pastor when he preaches (most of the time), but at the sermon's end, things seem to back up.

That's the time when the whole thing becomes a ritual. Open your song books to page so and so—please rise—if you want to be saved come forward—if you want to straighten things out come to the altar—or if you'd like to join the church come forward. Then if someone joins we all file past and shake hands and then go home. Is that ritual or not? We're just a group—not individuals with real needs, joys, or pains. Are we serious or do we play games?

I sat in church Wednesday night and wondered why I came. Now, I'm very impressed with all the college degrees floating around and all the abundance of Bible knowledge, plus the tremendous memories for gobs of scripture—but I can't really say I gained a thing spiritually.

When it comes down to it, I felt mentally deprived as I left. Not to mention the fact that I felt terribly uneasy while I sat there. I felt that at any moment I might be called upon and then my ignorance would be put on display. If I'm in a minority I should go elsewhere I guess, but I don't know where I'd go. Surely a church as large as Zion Hill could meet the needs of those lacking in college degrees or the opportunities to have attended Bible colleges.

November 30

Eugene made a remark that set my wheels to turning. He said something about trying to understand my moods because of all I've been through these past months. It occurred to me that in a disagreement with me, he's at a disadvantage. He can't say too much because in the event that I should get ill again he'd feel guilty and have trouble living with himself. That's one more problem that I don't know how to solve.

This past year has been rough for me and almost equally so for him. I try not to be so wrapped up in me that I forget the family. I do think I'm doing better and that I owe to my Saviour.

December 6

In all, I've seen 12 different doctors this past year. Out of the 12 I'd say three actually care. I felt good from the time I went to the hospital about the first of November until this past week.

Amy has been about to drive me up a wall with her constant complaining. If I didn't have Eugene to come home to, I couldn't go on. He's my earthly shelter.

We've had some beautiful sunsets lately which show the majesty of our Creator. I mentioned how beautiful they were to a cashier and she looked at me as if I were crazy. Then she said, "No, I don't have time." What a pity.

December 8

Today has been another nice Sunday. This evening James portrayed Joseph in the Christmas play put on by the Junior boys and girls. I guess these programs are strictly for the audience because the kids generally are in shock, to say the least.

December 9

Today started out okay but it turned sour. My neck began to

bother me on the left side. I don't understand why and it makes me very tense.

I came home to find the house in a real mess and I went into a rage. Eugene had been home all day and I felt he could have done better.

I've kept the job mainly because of the insurance. Whether Eugene realizes it or not I do it for his benefit. I don't feel so great that I would work every day by choice. Maybe it's expecting too much for Eugene and the kids to do their own picking up, but this much I know—I can't work all day and come home and work half the night, too. Maybe today is one of those days that I need a good cry.

To top it off, Marilyn called me and was telling me how distraught Mom is. Marilyn was crying about Mom and her situation. Lord, forgive me, but I couldn't see beyond me. Not less than 30 minutes earlier I'd sat in the bathroom and cried till I couldn't cry anymore and I wondered how long it would take me to bleed to death if I slit my wrists. I'm making no apologies because when I wallow in self-pity, it's just on paper.

December 11

Another doctor's office—Pap test. The doctor said everything was fine as far as he could tell. He said I looked fine and had a healthy attitude. He was proud of the way I was coping emotionally. If I've made emotional progress, then it doesn't have a whole lot to do with what I can do but what I'm able to do with God's help, mostly His help.

I know He wants to use me and will if I make myself available. I was being honest when I told the doctor I was surprised to be alive. If the Lord plans to use me wouldn't it be wonderful knowing that I was able to do something special?

It's been almost a year since I got the news of the cancer and I've countless ups and downs, but my Saviour has been just what He promised. Although I don't laugh a whole lot I still have joys untold and contentment that only comes from above.

December 14

It's a strange thing about pity—sometimes I want it and sometimes I bitterly resent it. The doctor commented that it had been almost a year and I was still alive. He was trying to be encouraging, but I kept feeling that strong undercurrent of pity. Sometimes that makes me uneasy.

I told the doctor about the man who was selling cancer insurance at school. When he found out that I'd had cancer he told me that 44% of cancer patients are completely cured. Now, I know he was trying to be encouraging, but we both know that leaves 56% who don't make the cured list.

The doctor pointed out that while people made unfeeling remarks to me, they probably did the same to Eugene. I hadn't thought about that.

I told the doctor that I felt I'd have been better off if I hadn't seen those doctors downtown. He said it was probably best that I had. He wasn't there and I didn't go into detail about the way I was handled. Why can't I just drop it? I can't because come what may I'll never forget it. It left an emotional scar that nothing can erase.

I think I come nearer to being honest with myself now, and therefore more honest with God. When it comes right down to it, I know lots of people who are more to be pitied than me. Why can't I do a better job of reaching out? Help me, Lord, to start at home.

December 15

I read some this evening and talked at length with Eugene. I feel it's important that he and I keep communication lines open—now more than ever. I want him to feel free to act and react as much as possible as he always has. It's too much of a strain trying to avoid anger, to keep everything sweetness and light. It's not normal for him or me.

December 16

I'm reading another book on the Jews of Poland. I can hardly believe the things that took place. It makes my own life seem like a bed of roses. So few of us have even a slight idea of what it's like to suffer.

Jerrie Caine, who was in the hospital with me in 1974, was telling me that her Mom has the lump. It is strange the way our lives weave in and out with others. Jerrie's mother is a fine person. I really like her—even better than I do Jerrie. I sensed compassion and caring in both of them but particularly in her mother. I know some of the things that are going through her mind and I can readily sympathize with her.

December 17

Each day brings me closer to a Christmas I didn't think I'd live to see. This past year makes this Christmas very special in many ways, starting with the birth of Christ. Christmas is more real because Christ is more alive to me now than He has been in the past.

Another thing that makes this year more special is that things don't mean as much. After all, what are things? Can they guarantee health or can things assure me of eternal life? Now I'm forced to look more clearly at life. I know that I'm not promised or assured of a tomorrow so why shouldn't I be careful about right now? God gave His Son, and I'm glad. He did, more so this year than ever before. Each day of my life I'm more aware of how much Jesus loves me and it never ceases to amaze me that He should care so much. I'm so glad that He does.

December 18

My friend Laura commented that Christmas lost its joy when she found out about Santa. I said I didn't remember ever believing in Santa nor did I teach that to my children. She told me that was awful.

Why is it awful to be truthful with children? I never tried to make my children believe that the stories of "Cinderella," "Red Riding Hood," or "Snow White" were anything other than stories of fantasy. Why should it be any different with Santa Claus? Whether he's real or not doesn't alter the reality of Christmas one bit. So I don't consider it earth shattering to learn that Santa Claus isn't real.

Christmas is wonder because our Saviour was born. God gave us more than Santa ever could. A sack of toys doesn't compare with eternal life.

December 19

It's strange how I go for a long time without anyone asking probing questions and then suddenly the questions start. It happened twice today—first with Amy and then with Bertha G. Amy asked me if I felt that I was cured. I told her I didn't know. I had to make adjustments to not knowing and that was the most difficult part. She commented that my faith helped, but she could never know how much.

Then I met Bertha and she said she was concerned and wanted to know what the doctors thought. When people come right out and ask I usually answer like they ask (outright). I told her and she got tears in her eyes. Sometimes I'm not sure whether a person's reaction is compassion, shock, or just curiosity.

December 21

Rini, Marilyn and I went for a drive together. The company was great. We enjoyed the outing.

I anticipate each day, expecting something special. My life has changed in many ways this year. Slowly I'm learning to embrace each day and to get as much from it as possible.

I've turned my face into icy rain and felt glad to be able to feel it; I've turned my body to the cold blowing wind and felt sheer joy as it whipped through my hair and made my coat flap about me. I've cried from despair, then felt the despair turn to relief as I took time to notice how tears felt rolling gently down my face. Yes, I've learned to embrace each day and all the emotions that a day brings because that's part of living and while I live I want all that God has to offer.

December 23

The probing of last week just unraveled me. Sometimes I can take it and sometimes I can't handle the pressures. I guess I'll know I've come a long way when someone asks an unfeeling question that I can take in stride.

Once again Preacher Hays has been willing to listen and give sensible suggestions. I must remember what he said about God not needing any help. It's funny how you can be so close to a situation that you don't see obvious things. I had been hesitant to give God as much credit as He should have been getting, because I kept thinking that if I died it would appear that God had failed. Preacher Hays said God didn't need my help, and he was right. I didn't resent his pointing it out.

Tonight Eugene found a knot or lump on James' neck. It alarmed me quite a bit but, dear God, help me to trust You and not cross bridges before I get to them.

December 24

It seems I've lived a lifetime in the year since last Christmas. I'm amazed that I'm fairly sane and even feeling good if I discount the physical problems that I'll have until Jesus replaces this body with a really good one. My Saviour has done wonders with me this year. He's picked me up when there was no way I could have gone any further by myself. He's shown me the way when I was sure there wasn't any way. I don't need anyone's pity and I don't indulge in self-pity too frequently. When I do, it usually has something to do with the cancer starting over rather than the problem with the stiffness and soreness in my neck or the problem with my tongue. Will my faith ever get strong enough so that I'll completely trust the Lord?

The doctor thinks James' lump is a swollen lymph gland. He put him on some antibiotics. I'm reminded that I have a Saviour who knows what He's doing and He's perfectly capable of looking after James, come what may.

December 26

We went to Rini and Rick's. Eugene, Jack, Marilyn and Mom helped them load up their belongings once more. Tomorrow they'll move to Florida. I suspect they'll both be happier there.

Eugene and I spent the evening listening to music. I enjoyed Eugene's presence and the music without doing anything else at the same time. The preacher must have been praying for me because I haven't felt so relaxed in a long time. Idle moments in the past few months have had a tendency to drive me up a tree instead of relaxing me. I was actually able to sit around, talk, and just do nothing and not get strung out. I can hardly believe it.

Today was really beautiful and I'm not talking about the weather. It was filled with serene moments. That to me is joy.

December 27

We kept Nessie and Sue while Marilyn and Jack helped Rini and Rick move. We had a good time playing charades. Eugene's been home, and I laid on the couch while we spent the whole day talking.

December 29

The sermon at church today seemed to be for me especially. I'm not so naive as to think that the sermon only applied to me but I'm sure that quite a bit was for me though not intentional on the Preacher's part. We've had some fine pastors before but I feel immensely blessed at this time to be a member of Zion Hill. Maybe it's because the Lord touched my life more than once in a special way. I've been able to talk freely to Preacher Hays when it was imperative that I talk to someone. I don't know why I've been able to talk to him like I do unless it was meant to be. Sometimes I feel sorry for myself, then I can't help but take stock, and then I know how blessed I am.

We went to the airport to pick up Marilyn and Jack. The airport is an exciting place to me even when I am not flying. Eugene likes it too. Marilyn is another of those people who I feel very blessed in having as a part of my life.

December 30

I still frequently feel apart from the human race. Why do I feel so separate? I have so many questions and too few answers. I can't confide in others often because they have no way of knowing what I'm talking about.

Even the doctors frequently misunderstand what I'm asking. Am I so vague? Perhaps I don't make myself clear and that's why I often resort to being blunt. I know that sometimes people think I'm unnecessarily blunt, but when they don't grasp what I'm saying, what else can I do but be plain?

Sometimes people can't cover their expressions quickly enough and I catch their looks of pity turning to shock, then to unbelief. As people often do, they dismiss something they're afraid to think about. It's okay for them to pry into the depths of my feelings but they quickly cover their own. Instead of asking questions like, "Do you think you're cured?" why don't they ask themselves why they're curious about it? Who's the concern for, me or themselves? Maybe some day I'll develop a thicker skin. I love life, most of the time, just like anyone else, but I don't have any supernatural powers.

December 31

Imagine, the last day of 1974, and I'm not only alive but well, thanks to a Saviour who cares. It's true I've had moments of extreme distress but I've also had moments of peacefulness, excitement, and many of the emotions that go with living. Soon I'll accept the fact that it doesn't matter how long one lives but how one lives. I'm always remembering that book title *A Time In the Sun*. The book is about Indians, and one of them says, "Each man has his time in the sun." It struck me as a very beautiful thing.

I hope to see some real improvements in myself in the coming year. While I live, surely I should make all the improvements possible, but without the help of God I can't accomplish anything. So many times I forget where my help comes from and then I feel panic-stricken.

January 2, 1975

Today is Eugene's 32nd birthday. I have known him 16 years. I can hardly believe that so much has happened in 16 years. I regret that I haven't been a better wife in the 14 years that we've been married. If I could reach back I would make quite a few changes, but the Lord willing, I'll do better with the time that's left.

I went to the woods and tramped around behind Eugene as he showed me something that is dear to his heart. It's strange the different things that give pleasure. I suppose Eugene experiences some of the same joys in the woods that I get from music and books.

78

January 3

Chalk up another lazy, wonderful day. I didn't do much of anything but enjoyed the day nevertheless. I visited Pat Henley for the first time in a good while. I don't believe I've ever felt bored while I was with Pat and yet I don't really know what the attraction is.

I had an interesting conversation with Elsa Kidd tonight. People are reaching out all around us. Why can't we all be more honest, loving and just plain caring? So many of our problems could become lighter if we shared. So often I've been unwilling to listen or for that matter unwilling to talk.

January 5

I can hardly believe it but I've actually been able to relax these two weeks. I've enjoyed my Christmas holidays just sitting around a good bit totally relaxed. But alas, tomorrow the routine begins again.

With the Lord's help I'm going to lick this problem of letting people unnerve me with their gross remarks. I get most of these remarks at school from supposedly professional people.

January 6

I not only arose at the wee hour of 6:30 but managed to get ready for school and leave without undue disaster.

Amy voluntarily told me that she wanted to start going to church again and had talked to her husband about it. Lord, if You're dealing with her, help me not to do anything to mess up the process. I'd like to help her, but someone else might be more helpful. Then again, I'm the one that's here, so why not me?

January 10

Marilyn, Betty, Nessie and I went to Conyers to shop after supper at Marilyn's. We got into a bit of tornado weather. As we were standing in the store, watching the wind rattle the plate glass windows, it hit me that I wasn't in the least afraid. If I could conquer my fear of pain like I have other fears, I'd have it made. I would say nagging fear keeps me humble, but I don't seem to fall in that category.

A year ago today, following the major surgery, I was somewhat out of it. In some ways it doesn't seem like a year, but in many ways it seems like a lifetime. I've aged many years in a lot of ways. Obviously I have quite a bit more gray hair but the new wrinkle is that I feel removed from people most of the time. I'm reasonably sure that regardless of the length of my life I'll never be the same again. I don't think the same. It's odd that I'm more tolerant about some things and completely without patience about others.

January 12

Although the rain poured outside, the sun shined inside. I love Sundays—they've become days of rest and refreshment. Special prayers must have gone up for me about relaxing because I've done much better lately.

My Sunday that the Lord has so graciously supplied has begun to gently close its doors so now I'll accept another of the gifts from above—sleep.

January 14

Tonight I went to a baby shower for Preacher Hays' daughter. Ordinarily I don't attend showers because I don't like them. I went because I think so much of Preacher and Mrs. Hays.

January 15

Mrs. Hanson suggested that we cultivate the habit of remembering that Christ lives in us. I'm listening to one of her tapes.

Today I walked into the lounge and two teachers were discussing mortgage insurance. One said, "The lack of it is worse than a dreaded disease like cancer." Can you imagine comparing the loss of material goods to having cancer and then concluding that the loss of things is worse?

January 16

My lips crack and peel until I wonder that there's any skin left. I'm beginning to doubt that the glands will ever work any better. The thought crossed my mind that some day none of them would be working. Then I was horrified. If I go on thinking along those lines I'll end up thinking about a quickie death, and I'm not being flip. I could feel sorry for me without applying any effort. It's strange, but I feel driven to write down all my feelings.

Sometimes I want to close myself away from everybody. Once more I don't see life here as too special. Maybe I've seen, heard and felt too much this year for I don't cling to life as much as I have in the past. I don't like what I see in the mirror and what I sometimes see in people's faces. I don't always like what I've heard people say, or the tones of their voices. I didn't like the sound of my own crying, or the sound of my voice cutting someone short for no reason.

Now about the things I've felt—mental and physical pain— it doesn't ever stop and no one knows or understands. I don't dare go into detail. Dear God, it's become a part of me. Will it get any better? I ask that, then pray it won't get worse. I understand suicide where physical pain is involved. I'm tempted almost daily. Unlike the great saints, I can't (yet) rejoice in whatever state I'm in. I accept it, but not joyfully.

January 17

Tonight I find contentment—isn't that crazy? I never know what to expect of myself. My moods change frequently and rapidly. Someone suggested that the medicine might be responsible. I still have the same problems and I'm not on medicine now.

January 19

Once more my Sunday has slipped away from me. I get so much from Sundays that I consider the whole day a special gift. God knew I'd need Sunday so He set it aside, and for that I'm so thankful. There was a time that I requested special weather for Sundays but now I'm usually just glad it's Sunday. Thank You, Lord, for Your special nearness today as I sat reading Your Word. I felt so thrilled that I felt the tears on my face before I even thought about them. I felt Your presence so strongly.

January 20

Today has been quite a mixture—good and bad. I truly love

some of those kids at school. Jerry frequently tells me he loves me and hugs my neck so hard that it hurts, but I would never push him away.

Along with the pleasures come the not-so-good moments. At one time during the day Amy came past me and said, "Your lips are bleeding—what's the matter?" I just said the dryness made them get chapped. Cracking, peeling, and now bleeding. What next? Oh, God, I'm strung out.

My own strength doesn't even get me halfway through the day. For some stupid reason I wait until my fright turns to terror before I listen, then, Lord, You quietly fold me in Your love and give me what I've needed all day. You'd think after this past year I'd be the first to realize I can't go it alone. Why do I persist in trying to carry a burden that I cannot possibly handle?

I guess Satan has a heyday with me at times. I try not to underestimate him but, like many, I fall into his trap and get in trouble.

Lord, I don't know why You love me, but I'm so glad You do. So often I'm blinded by tears before I see clearly, then once more I stand amazed at such love. I'm surrounded by it and once more I feel safe. If I could sing a beautiful song of adoration I would, right now. Since I can't do that I'll say, "I love You so much."

Once again, I'm listening to Jack Holcomb singing, "I asked the Lord to comfort me," and I could never explain just how much the song has meant to me this year.

> I asked the Lord to comfort me
>   when things weren't going my way;
> He said to me, "I will comfort you,
>   and lift your cares away."

I know that my Saviour has used many Christians to lift my spirits many, many times this past year.

January 22

I'm reading a book on guilt and grace and I understand all too well what the author is talking about. He has a section on time and guilt. That's certainly not a small thing with me. I often worry about not using my time wisely. I didn't go to church tonight and I feel some guilt, but not too much. I was more interested in the book the preacher loaned me than the slides taken in Canada. The preacher won't be there tonight either, but when he's not there a very special part is missing.

I suppose at different times in one's life different people are special, depending on the situation. I'd say Eugene, Marilyn and Preacher Hays have headed my list for this past year. All this would probably sound trivial to some but I find it imperative to be honest with myself. I suspect when a person discovers that death could be a here-and-now thing instead of a remote possibility it affects his way of thinking.

January 23

Rick and Rini might come up this weekend—it would be nice if they could. I don't know how Rini can work all week and then travel on the weekends. She must have a lot more energy than I do. I wish they'd both been able to stay in town. It would've been good for Mom and Dad, and then Rini's just a lot of fun.

January 24

Marilyn and Jack came over tonight. After shopping at the mall, Marilyn and I sat in the bedroom and just talked for a good two hours. She's so easy for me to talk to. It must be good therapy because I feel good while talking with her, and afterwards too. I can talk to her about how I feel without being under pressure.

January 27

I was nauseated all the way to the clinic today. It's from tension because it happens every trip. Dr. Williams said everthing was fine as far as he could tell.

I was disappointed when I went to Radiology and was met by a different doctor. Dr. McRae said that Dr. Bostwick had gone to Tennessee. I was stunned; I felt betrayed. Dr. Bostwick had seemed very interested in my welfare. Then I discover he left without so much as a good-by.

I read an article that said it was important for a patient to have confidence in her doctor. It shows me that I should put my confidence in One who will never leave me nor forsake me. (Thanks, Lord, I needed that.) How many times do I have to be reminded? Sometimes it's very difficult to keep in mind what I know in my heart.

It's distressing to go to the clinic and see what you see, not to mention what you hear. For example, the doctor spoke to an elderly lady who walked down the hall. Then he asked the nurse, "Did you see the lady I saw? I thought she would be dead and gone by now." Will I ever hear remarks like that and not cringe?

Mom had her surgery today and it was more extensive than they thought it would be. She was feeling okay tonight; I hope she sleeps well. I suppose they'll send the tissues off to the lab. Maybe tomorrow they'll know something about it. Dear God, please don't let it be cancer.

January 28

Nothing was said about Mom's pathology findings so I suppose everything's fine.

An experience with the doctor really put me in a down mood. The doctors have socked it to me almost to the point of being brutal, so there's no way on God's earth that I could come to the conclusion that my situation isn't serious. Okay, considering all that, why do they say things to a point then vaguely hint around? For example, the doctor says, "I can't find anything but I can't tell about the scar tissue. That's encouraging, but live each day to the utmost."

Now this is the way I hear it: "I can't find any lumps on the left side of your neck but I don't want to be responsible for building any false hopes, so I must point out that there could be lumps I can't feel on the other side around the scar. In case I'm wrong and your life span is considerably shorter than I'd hope, well whoop it up each day you do have."

Now I'm reasonably intelligent and am well aware that they can't be positive that the cancer is not spreading. I wouldn't blame them if it was; they've helped all they could, but I wish they'd handle the visits differently. The doctor could say, "I don't feel anything and that's good. Do you have any questions or problems? If not, I'll see you next trip."

If a good mental attitude is that important in a patient, then why can't the doctor help lift patients instead of burying them? Above all things they shouldn't throw percentages at them. I don't care which category the patient falls in—when a person's been told he has cancer he more than likely would put himself in the low percentage group.

January 29

I talked with Preacher Hays a little after prayer meeting. He told me about a lady at Clayton General Hospital with cancer. He wanted to find out more about her and if she wanted to talk to someone. He asked if I wanted to talk to her. I don't know what I'd say, but I sure know quite a few things I wouldn't say. I can certainly guess at what she's feeling. Lord, how well I know.

January 30

When most people ask me how I feel I usually say "Fine," and let it go at that. I'm not laying myself wide open for questions unless I feel capable of coping.

I asked Mom tonight if she'd heard any report about the lab work. She said she didn't see any need to rock the boat. I was surprised that she didn't ask. I always wanted to know even though I wasn't always pleased with what they found.

January 31

Another month ends and I'm still alive. How about that? I may appear to be down, but the fact that I usually write before bedtime might account for some of it. After all, by that time I've generally gone about as far as I can go. Under normal circumstances a person is somewhat drained. For some reason, I've felt extremely dizzy today.

Today at lunch one of the assistants was telling about an experience when she was a medical receptionist. A nurse was involved with the doctor. The assistant said that she lost her job because of it. Then she added that later the doctor called her and wanted her to come back to work because the nurse was in the hospital. To quote her (the assistant) she said, "The nurse was eat up (here she paused and looked at me, then added) with it, and she died."

Now here I could have asked just what she was eat up with, leprosy, bubonic plague or cancer maybe? Why didn't I? I must feel it would be useless.

I've gone through all sorts of changes since last May. I can't back up to January '74 because after the surgery everyone was optimistic. Then the physical pain probably outweighed the mental pain. In May the mental part was worse by far, and then during the treatments the physical pain was worse than before too.

In the first stage I was trying to come to a conclusion about which type of suicide I'd take. In the next I was struggling with God, seeing what He would do, I could do, or what we could do. It's a funny thing I never did get too sure about that.

For a while I felt that if I didn't have a suitable amount of faith I'd die because of the lack of it. Somewhere I came up with the idea that whether I got any pat answers or not didn't change anything. I have some certainties and that's all the Lord has seen fit to endow me with. One of those certainties is that I do have the assurance this very moment that Jesus loves me and cares about me and whatever tomorrow brings or doesn't bring He'll still love, care and look after me like any loving parent. In fact He'll even do more because His powers surpass those of an earthly parent.

I get very upset when I think people aren't being honest with me. To me it's much better to come right out than to hint around. If people want to say, "How are you?" that's fine. But not this way (I've had it happen): "How are you? Does everything seem okay?" One, everything in all my life has never seemed okay. Number two, if they mean the cancer, they should know that I really don't know. Number three, suppose I had received terrible reports, would they want me to answer them bluntly on the side-walk or in the grocery store? Maybe I should wear a sign around my neck saying, "I'm a child of the King: He created the world and He's looking after me."

February 1

The children and I went shopping with Mom and Dad. Mom

86

thought I could eat a candy bar without drinking something with it. Since the treatments I can't eat anything without something to drink with it. I'm constantly drinking so I won't get a sore throat. Sometimes when I wake up in the morning my lips look like I got sun-burned and have started to peel, and at times my lips bleed.

February 2

At church tonight I asked the preacher about the lady he told me about and he said they would do some biopsies and more tests. I've had her on my mind ever since he told me about her.

Dear God, my heart really goes out to people like us for many reasons. First, I know the importance of knowing Jesus as personal Saviour. Then following that, are many adjustments even if they're temporary. Even knowing Christ I wasn't without fear when I was told the facts, nor am I now. I still have fear-filled moments—notice I said moments. When I'm extremely afraid one moment and then suddenly the fear is gone, who else but my Saviour could have intervened?

I would like to be able to help others who have cancer, but I'm not sure how. At first I thought I'd have to live at least five or six years after having cancer. But when I think about it maybe it's more important to help reach people as soon as they've been told. If you wait, they have time to get panic-stricken.

As for me, I have made some positive adjustments. Now I know how to go quickly to the Lord when things get beyond me. Now I know that without Him I'm nothing and would see everything as hopeless. Now I know from experience what He can do if I but ask.

February 3

James has gone skating, Betty's in her room, and Eugene is on the phone, and I have the whole den to myself. So rarely am I alone that I hardly know what to do with myself. The quietness is heavenly.

I have had the lady the preacher told me about on my mind all day. I hope she's better. Hopefully, she'll get it all together and won't have to dip in and out of despair like I did, and sometimes still do. I'm just thankful I'm not hitting rock bottom.

It bothers me that I don't have any desire to talk about the future. Now is more important than a tomorrow that may not come. I have no inclination to make plans for next year. Do I down deep think I'll be dead? I don't think I know. Maybe I've done a super job of suppressing. I told Pat H. this past weekend that I don't have any deep-down feeling about whether or not I'll make it. She led up to this by saying she has nothing but good feelings concerning me. I wasn't upset as I talk with Pat with ease. It could be because she is always positive. Bless her heart, she was on the verge of tears when I told her I had considered suicide. I think many people consider suicide at one time or another with less reason than I've had. So why should it come as a surprise?

Here I pointed out some of the saints who died rather rough deaths. I hate to shoot her theory full of holes, but it is true. Preacher Hays pointed that out to me a long time ago. Even skipping the part about the saints, I don't measure up to all that goodness and I doubt if Ellen does. Not that I think Ellen isn't a good person—I'd say better than average. But let's face it, that doesn't mean roses in abundance forever. As for myself, if my life span depended on my goodness—well!

Anyway, I love Pat and don't mind talking in depth to her or answering her questions because I know she loves me and only asks questions because she cares about me, not from vulgar curiosity.

Eugene is super. He wants to give me the world, and would if he could. I adore the way he says "cancer" when that's what he means. I don't think I could accept anything less from him. I can excuse lack of honesty coming from others but not from Eugene —not while we live together. Afterthought: By my expression, "I adore the way he says 'cancer,' " I mean not the way he says it, but the way he doesn't avoid the word. When people go to such great lengths to avoid saying cancer, I get a sick feeling in my tummy and I want to scream "Say it, say it, say it—CANCER!"

February 4

I'm watching a movie on TV, "Death Be Not Proud." It's

about a boy with a brain tumor. It starts with the boy having his hair shaved. Like me, he joked about it. I remember all too well how I felt although it wasn't my whole head. It's strange how people joke when they'd really like to scream.

The boy, like me, connected flowers with death. Although it's been a year and a half since the surgery, I still abhor artificial flowers and feel almost the same towards cut flowers. I only feel pleasure in looking at flowers when they're growing free and easy. When I was a kid I remember looking forward to seeing daisies in bloom. My brothers, my sister and I used to run through them and lie down in them trying to hide from one another. Guess where they grew in such profusion? In a cow pasture. I could stand amidst them and see daisies all around—such beauty.

The boy in the movie also worried about wasting time. (It's a true story.) He also lashed out from time to time. People without problems frequently feel hostile, so why should people always be telling a patient to take it easy if the patient expresses hostility. The boy told his parents not to keep asking how he feels.

The boy died in the end. His father said death took him like a thief. His mother said she accepted it and hoped they'd leave behind them what he had, a love of love. The worst tragedy was that they only had hope while he lived and after death nothing. I watched the movie and didn't feel torn apart. I have come a long way. Not that I didn't feel the same emotions that I've felt before, but one was missing—hopelessness. I didn't say that because I have any of those prophecy type feelings but because I honestly know it's not hopeless nor will it ever be.

February 5

Tossing and turning as I did last night starts the day off all wrong. I was alone this evening so I just cried my heart out. My tears got the bedspread wet and I didn't even feel better.

I've thought so much about the lady the preacher told me about, I asked again how she was. He said she wasn't much better. I told him I probably couldn't help her much anyway because I'm up and down too much myself. If the lady talked about suicide, what could I say? That I wouldn't do it? I wouldn't bet on it. I don't know for sure what I will or won't do. If she felt hostile or bitter, what could I say? I'm quite familiar with both feelings. I have wonderful peace at times but I also have bitter torment at times. Never for a moment can I dismiss all the horrible possibilities of the cancer that I might still have. I couldn't tell her she shouldn't feel this or that because I've felt it all in regards to the horror, unbelief, hopelessness. I am always aware that the physical pain can get worse, lots worse. At first I said I'd die before I'd go back in a hospital, but I'd have to wait and see.

February 6

I've been taking valium so frequently that my whole body is out of whack. I have a back problem and I don't know if that's a strained muscle or my lung. Dear God, will I develop something new every week? It would be easier to quit worrying if these physical things would quit cropping up.

I want to trust and take one day at a time but I can only do this sometimes. I keep thinking I should be doing better—that I should have made more progress. Why haven't I? I feel that resorting to the valium is like backsliding, not really relying on the Lord. Am I cracking up? Sometimes I think I am. The doctor at the hospital always says if you need help before appointment time, call and come in. I feel guilty asking him to spend time on me when I see others in worse shape. It's true I have physical pain often and mental frustrations like crazy but I'm not sure he could help me.

February 8

I have been listening to one of Mrs. Hanson's tapes. I feel upset because I can't put myself in any of the categories she talks about. I tried to explain this to Eugene and he didn't understand why this should upset me. Why shouldn't I be upset if I listen to tape after tape, read gobs of books on being *God's Woman, Total Woman, Fascinating Womanhood,* take the tests and fail? Instead of feeling better I feel depressed, and feel like a failure.

Eugene and James walked over the land today and Betty and I, Marilyn and her girls walked and walked for miles at the mall. During this time I didn't feel uptight. I was relaxed, but my mind was busy. Maybe I should enroll in the next quarter at the junior college, but adding more work might be too much. Maybe the preacher will clearly show me some answers tomorrow.

Lord, am I asking too much when I want special miracles now? I picked up another book in the book store and the doctor who wrote the book talked about how desperately patients with cancer need help to handle the mental strain. I agree one hundred percent.

It's odd to me that I can keep control over my emotions on the job yet when I'm home I find myself frequently on the verge of tears. I don't cry in front of the kids but only when I'm alone or sometimes when I'm with Eugene. He may wonder what is going on too, because until this year the times I cried were few. I have really made up for it. Am I any better off by spilling my tears? It hasn't made Eugene feel any better. He must think I'm strung out because he suggested that I start smoking again. That's odd— why start that now when I hardly ever think about it any more? I'm puzzled every way I turn. I strongly feel the urge to take off all alone. I guess I'm hunting solace in the wrong places.

February 9

Revival services started at church today. It's kinda strange the way things work. Eugene wasn't a Christian when we got married and I hadn't been to church in a long time. Then I heard that a former pastor our family had loved was preaching at a revival service at a church not far away. Thus, in that manner, I turned back to God and not long afterwards Eugene accepted Christ. I can see God's hand in so many things.

February 11

Hello, today's my birthday—31—over the hill—strung out —the whole bit. I get down and switch moods back and forth so much that it's beginning to frighten me. How can I be in control in the morning, sometimes up until late in the afternoon, and then start going to pieces? What happens between morning and afternoon? I'm beginning to suspect that I'm more at ease at school than at home.

Dear God, how I need help. At times I've felt such unreal peace —that was You, God wasn't it? Then what about all those other times when I'm far from peaceful? Have those peaceful moments compensated for the agony, terror and aloneness?

February 12

Was it 15 years ago today that I quietly left school, stood at the top of the steps a few seconds before Eugene drove up, then went to North Georgia and got married? In those few seconds I almost went back inside. What if I had?

Eugene said we had quite a thunderstorm last night, but I slept straight through it—I didn't even wake up for water. Am I wrong to think God knows when I'm reaching the end of what I can endure? Several people at school talked about the storm, but I slept. Ordinarily I wake up before Eugene does, but not so last night.

I enjoy going to church but it's not easy to work till 3:30, come home and work till 7:00 and then go to church till 9:00 or later.

February 13

I talked with Marilyn on the phone after I got in from church. She commented that she liked to talk to me because I was jolly. I told her that it had something to do with her because ordinarily I'm not jolly with other people, not even Eugene. He doesn't bring out the best in me, nor I him. I dare say I'm not the right woman for Eugene. But after 15 years what do you do? Even after Mrs. Hanson's tapes, I can't seem to make the necessary improvements. How can I find plenty of things to talk about with Marilyn and not so with Eugene? Oh, I could rattle on about trivial matters but I can't stand conversations like that. They make me nervous. I don't know what the answer is.

February 14

This has really been one rushed week—I don't think I could go through two weeks like this. I'm utterly exhausted and I have hardly touched this house all week, I'm dreading my trip to the dentist—I don't like having my mouth even touched much less worked on.

I've sat through a revival and it's been good, but I feel as I often do, that it's not geared to me and my problem. I'm really glad that people have been saved and others have straightened out their problems. So often when I read or when I hear someone different I think I'm gonna find some answers to living with this situation, but there was nothing for me, just as in other times. How can I get answers from people who haven't felt as I've felt? They wouldn't begin to know the agony a person goes through.

It's strange the way people single me out to tell about the latest cancer victim. I was cornered once again by a parent and guess what she wanted to tell me about? Right, a friend of hers was in the hospital and the doctors thought he had cancer. Why me? She could have told Amy V. just as easily, but no, I was the one who got the details. The evangelist talked about the verse that says all things work out for the good of those who love the Lord. He was exactly right, but that's very hard for me to grasp at times.

February 16

I'm worried about the trouble with my back. It could be a strained muscle or my lung.

I get upset out of proportion to the situation and then sometimes it takes several hours for me to be sensible about it. This is not only bad for me but I fear that it will eventually ruin my relationship to Eugene.

February 17

Amy wasn't going to be at school today so I went to work even though I didn't feel like it. I went by the doctor's office after school and he said my lungs sounded fine. He said I'd probably strained a muscle. I'm to take muscle relaxers and not to lift anything with my right hand—not even my pocketbook. He also suggested that I put my arm in a sling around the house.

He said the tablets might make me sleepy but I can't feel any effect from them. That's fine because if they'd make me sleepy I couldn't work and take them.

I hated not going to church yesterday. Sunday seems so meaningless when I don't go. I finished reading most of the evangelist's books.

Lisa started questioning me at school today. "How do you know you're cured?" What more can I say when I explain what's been done and people still ask. I guess they can't conceive of living with such a positive uncertainty about life or death. Everybody does, but everybody doesn't realize it the way I do. I hear a lot of Christian people say that they do, but they really don't because they talk too much in terms of tomorrow and the way out future to really believe it.

February 18

I can take the tablets and work, too—they only make me sleepy. There's no danger because I take them right before I leave the house in the morning and by the time I get ready to drive back home they've worn off. I probably should stay home, but I hate to unless I have to.

If I can push myself and keep going physically, why can't I do as well mentally?

I never thought it would be so hard to remember not to lift anything. I'd feel silly wearing a sling as the doctor suggested, without a broken arm. Guess what—my Bible reading for today is that one about all things working out for good for those who love the Lord.

We've been having thunderstorms again. I never realized so many people were afraid of thunderstorms. At school that's all I've heard this week. This afternoon, after the kids had left, a storm came up rather suddenly and I had just walked over to the window and was watching the rain, wind and lightning when a teacher came by and questioned my standing alone watching the storm undisturbed. I can't remember ever being too alarmed over storms. What could lightning do to me that would be worse than the surgery or cancer? I'll leave the weather to God—after all, what can I do about it? I've often felt almost hypnotized while watching wind, rain, snow, hail and stormy seas. So many times this past year I've felt myself drawn to a window and caught myself gazing towards the heavens. It has a tranquilizing effect on me.

I wonder what happened to the lady the preacher told me

about. I've meant to ask but haven't had a chance. I'd just as soon not hear anything about people as to hear something and not hear anything else. It's like someone saying "Guess what?" and never finishing.

February 19

I rode to church tonight with Evelyn Stone. Dick White spoke in place of Preacher Hays. He was simple and direct and for my fuzzy mind that was great.

I wonder why the tablets make me sleepy. I'm looking forward to this weekend so I can give in to the medicine.

There's something about the church that I really love. I could get the same out of it by slipping in quietly alone and worshiping.

I feel rotten physically and fine mentally. My back felt much better this morning but no better tonight. I need to rest.

February 20

It will be seven months since the treatments stopped. It was five months last time before the cells started growing again. It's a privilege to be sane. I can still function reasonably. I'm not being flip—I'm really thankful. I have no idea how others who have have had cancer manage but I know some have lived long enough to find a way to stay sane. I've heard a few on TV talk about it, but they either hit it lightly or claim they weren't all that upset by it. As for the latter, well, people do lie, or maybe they just forget. That's one reason it's important to me to write down what I feel. Memory is often unreliable.

I talked with Jerrie Caine awhile ago and she said her Mom's lump had gone away. I was so relieved when James' went down. She also told me that the only way my back would get better, if it was a strained muscle, was to go to bed and let the muscle relaxers do their job. I think I'll call in tomorrow and stay home and rest.

February 21

I called the doctor and he suggested that I see a specialist. I'm not going to. The last time I saw a specialist it cost me $35 for about 20 minutes and he told me to turn up the radio to drown out the noise in my head. He'd probably tell me to pretend I didn't have a back.

I'm convinced Eugene missed his calling—he should have been a doctor. I told him this morning that I thought there was a knot by the scar and he suggested I put on a turtle-neck shirt and pretend I hadn't seen anything. That's what I call sound advice. I put on the turtle-neck shirt and feel much better about it. By using the same reasoning I can turn myself just so far and avoid hurting my back. That way I'll be rid of the back problem.

It's nice to be home without being rushed. I straightened the house and did the things I needed to do by about 10:30. I'm probably better off working because I'm not the type to devote hours to housecleaning. I do the essentials then find myself hunting something more interesting.

I've tried but I can't make myself friendly and outgoing. I can't see spending 15 minutes talking about flowers that boys give girls at dances, or boyfriends that a teacher had in elementary school. Good grief! The average conversation in the lounge is usually obscene or trivial. My saliva is too limited to waste on either one.

One of the teachers avoids me because she feels uncomfortable around me. I thought it might be because she has a horror of cancer but I was informed differently. Someone said she doesn't feel good about my relationship to God. I've never discussed my thoughts or feelings with her, although I have left the lounge when she started talking filthy. She's asked me a couple of times what I was reading. The books were by Christian authors but I didn't elaborate on what the books dealt with. The only time I can think of what I said was when I came back after the surgery. She commented that I was lucky. I told her that it was more than luck and that I felt the Lord had quite a bit to do with it. If that's true I hope it bothers her enough to make her do some soul-searching.

Today's been a beautiful day, outside and inside too. I've relaxed all evening. James came in from school, commented about how clean the house looked, and how he wished I didn't work. When I questioned him about it he said he liked it because then he wouldn't have to do any work. Some reason, huh?

February 22

Mr. Hanson called this morning and told Eugene that one of our deacons had died. I've gathered that he has been having a rough time for the last couple of years. I'm sure he's much better off now. I'm glad he wasn't in prolonged pain.

The thought came to me that I might soon be with him. I wonder if that's a normal thought or a premonition. When thoughts of death come to me now, I often wonder if this is some sort of premonition. I'm curious, not depressed. When Mr. Hanson called, I heard Eugene say, "Is that right?" and I knew someone had died. Then almost at once I knew it was the deacon. I feel so sorry for his wife and family. I'm sure that during times like this it has to be immensely comforting to know the love of God.

It helps, too, to think about the resurrection. Job said, "For I know that my redeemer liveth, and that he shall stand at the latter day upon the earth: And though after my skin worms destroy this body, yet in my flesh shall I see God." That is in Job 19:25 and 26.

February 23

I was curious about how Preacher Hays would handle the deacon's funeral. The preacher was brief and yet he said the right things. That was the first funeral I ever went to that didn't have that extreme feeling of abnormality. (It's hard for me to explain.) Sometimes the people seem to be in a trance. I breathed a sigh of relief when Preacher Hays talked in a normal way. I've heard so many preachers use unnatural phrases and sound so different, that it's no wonder that the whole atmosphere takes on that unreal quality. I'm not talking about the sound of emotion in someone's voice—I mean the phony sound.

February 24

I put in an appearance at PTA tonight but didn't stay because my back was hurting badly. I came home and took two of the muscle relaxers even though they burn my throat. But I was desperate. I've taken more medicine this past year than I did in the ten years before. I rarely even went to a doctor except when I was pregnant. I read that cancer patients spend enormous sums running to the doctor and I can see why. You're never sure whether to ignore an ache or run to the doctor because of it.

One of our parents had cancer last year. She was at PTA tonight. I've found her to be a very special person. I had one of her daughters in my class last year and the other one this year. Actually, she's the only person I know very well who has had cancer. She and I talked about it this past summer and a few times since school started. She told me tonight about her endless trips to doctors. She also mentioned how frightening it frequently is. She's a Christian and a Primitive Baptist.

February 25

Today during lunch one of the teachers asked if she could ask a personal question. I told her she could ask but I didn't know if I would answer. She wanted to know if any of my hair fell out during the treatments. The assistant that always gets in her two bits worth came up again with "How can you live and stay sane, not knowing?"

When people ask if they can ask a question, I begin to wonder if it'll be a different question or one I've heard dozens of times before. Maybe I should announce one day during lunch that I'm gonna declare it a question and answer session. Anyone can ask all the questions he wants to, no matter what they are, and after that they can't bring up the subject unless I mention it first.

Better still, I should write down all the questions I've been asked and answer them, then post them in the lounge and in our room, plus carry a copy around so that I could just hand it over when the situation arose.

I probably wouldn't get as many questions as I do if most people knew the whole story. I haven't gone into details with them.

Eugene says he thinks it bothers me more than I admit, when I'm questioned. Sometimes I know it bothers and sometimes not, depending on different things. For example, it depends on the way it's asked, who asks, and my mood at the moment.

The teachers at school don't know how pessimistic and dismal the doctors were when they examined me in June. They don't know that the doctors told me I'd have to have cobalt treatments, surgery that would involve removing half of my tongue, my jawbone on that side of my face, replacing it with some sort of pipe, and cleaning out my neck as far as they could go and leave me still alive. Thus I would be unable to talk, chew, or half swallow anything but mushy foods, not to mention being terribly disfigured. Then there would be a 75% chance that the cancer would start growing again. I didn't have that surgery, and by their standards I should be already dead, but for some reason, that only the Lord knows, I'm still alive.

Perhaps I should tell them the complete story but I can take the questions better than pity.

I know that the Lord loves and cares for me and I don't know how I could really get this across to them. If I say too much then, when I feel kinda down or depressed, they'll assume that God doesn't really love me or I'm not trusting Him like I say I do, or otherwise I wouldn't get depressed.

I'm still human and I don't know if they could understand or not. Maybe when I'm down, depressed or feeling rough, I'm the one who feels that God doesn't love or care for me. Is that why I avoid these in-depth conversations? In conversations, unlike in writing, I don't have time to carefully consider the questions or my answers.

My back hasn't bothered me as much today as yesterday. I didn't take any medicine during school and managed to get through the day.

I was thinking about not writing anymore, but if I don't do most of my complaining in here I might flag down some poor unsuspecting soul and bend his ears for hours.

This way I don't put stress on the saliva situation. Right now I'm taking muscle relaxers at night and grinding my teeth in the daytime.

February 26

Three days and the month is gone. I left my journals with the preacher tonight. It seems only yesterday I was in the hospital and decided to write down what I was feeling. This starts another notebook. I almost changed my mind about sharing them with him. Now that I did I feel tense about it. Why?

February 28

I went to the Kiwanis Club talent show at the Junior High tonight. Betty and Sarah rode their unicycles. I was pleasantly surprised when a young boy sang a religious song and won first prize. The judges could hardly do less after the audience-reaction applause.

March 3

I went to the clinic with my backache and apparently the cancer is spreading—I have a spot on my spine. I guess I've known all along that it would. I had the feeling yesterday that I shouldn't drive myself to the clinic but, typically, I ignored the warning signal and not only drove but took Betty and James with me.

As I was getting the latest information I said, "Well, God, I need You to get us home." We did make it. "Thanks, Lord."

I also had the feeling that I should leave the kids at home, but once again I ignored my feelings and took them with me.

I hate to admit it, Lord, but I don't think I'd mind being stoned right now. As a matter of fact I do feel like I got hit in the head with something. They gave me a treatment on my back today.

Isn't it funny—I had begun to think I was a hypochondriac and that the backache was in my mind and that perhaps I just wanted attention. It may be funny but I'm not laughing.

I made it home without losing control and then I cried all over the place. I've always admired real strength and courage. You'd think I could show a little, wouldn't you? Who knows—maybe it was strength just getting home without flying to pieces. As I sat there I kept saying to myself, "I'm not going to pieces, I'm not going to pieces." I guess the Lord was listening and He probably said, "Okay, Robin, you're not going to pieces—I'm right here and I'm going to get you out of this mess." He did. I remained calm and collected until I got home.

It takes me a while to get things together but I do, especially when time is limited. Perhaps I sound pessimistic but I don't see anything optimistic in what the doctors have told me. I'm not at all sure I ever should have allowed the first operation. I keep thinking I'd be better off if I'd stuck to my guns when I said No. Thank God, I did stick with my decision when I went to those doctors up town. I feel bad enough being told that today, without having gone through all that gross surgery. And now the doctor tells me it is growing in my spine.

I still think God is capable of miracles but don't suppose He's planning one—not what I have in mind, anyway. The Lord has presented me with a lot of different kinds of miracles and I mustn't forget this. I've had staggering blows five times this year and each time I've walked away reasonably composed.

Eugene asked me how I felt, and when I was slow to answer he asked, "Don't you want to talk about it?" I told him it was hard to answer that without thinking about it. I can't say I was really surprised.

I asked Dr. Williams how I was gonna stay sane. He said, "Trust in the Lord." I can't say I feel that everything is hopeless, I know better than that. I admit that I don't feel at all optimistic about the cancer. I have the thought of what this does to the family, especially Eugene. Never doubt, I hate what it does to me, too.

I looked out the window a while ago and saw the sun shining and birds flying through the air. I later commented to Eugene, "The audacity of the sun—it's shining brightly today." He didn't understand.

The world is once more falling in on me and all the while the sun shines brightly, birds fly gloriously through the air and flowers bloom and swing gently in the breeze. I know in my head that this happens all the time, but now it's my turn. I'm almost glad because I don't know how much more of the strain I could bear. After a while it does seem a relief.

Preacher Hays came by and once more I'm very thankful for him. I can talk to him without him throwing meaningless phrases plus strong hints of "holier than thou." Dear Lord, You know that would be more than I could bear. My world is reeling for sure now and my needs are greater than they've ever been. Help me to trust.

March 4

Back to the clinic today. Eugene took me this time. I had the bone scan and a treatment but didn't get the results. I'll have to wait—isn't that great? Dear God, I hope it's just in the one spot. At any rate I marvel at the power of God. I'm perfectly calm and I'm not on any medication right now. I'm not depressed—only God supplies peace like that. I talked with Preacher Hays about this and have decided not to tell the latest to the people at school and those at church except that I'll have some follow-up treatments. If I give out with all the information I'll put myself in for a lot of pity and I don't think I could take that.

Some time back I tried to put my feeling for Preacher Hays into words and it surprises me that that was really quite simple. I love him as a very dear Pastor and wish all Christians had pastors that cared as much.

I plan to go back to work and carry on as usual with a whole lot of help from my Saviour.

March 5

Eugene asked me yesterday how I felt. Let me say this. I feel like I would if I were hanging off the edge of a cliff and holding on only with my fingers. I think my fingers will give out any moment and then no way but down, down, down.

About the scan machine—I had to lie flat on my back for 45 minutes while the machine moved back and forth, up and down me while I remained as still as possible. The machine makes a terrific racket plus it comes so close to my nose that I thought it would knock it off. When I got through I asked the doctor if I might possibly have to do it again. He said it was highly unlikely. Guess what? In my case it was likely—I had to go under it again.

I figured that they found cancer all over my bones and that was the reason for the rerun. I didn't know the results until this evening. If I didn't believe in God I don't know how I'd have made it through the day. I kept thinking all day—how can things seem so normal and be so abnormal for me? Dear Lord, sometimes I feel as if I'm in a trance.

March 6

When I think back about the results of the test I'm not sure they were good or not. This way I have longer to dwell on it. I took the second treatment today and the machine was unbelievable. It would have made four out of the one they used before. Besides this, it was so loud I had to use earphones during the treatments. They'll alternate between the two machines. I'm feeling sick so I'm gonna try to go to sleep.

March 8

I feel as if I'm reaching for life and it's not there. My loved ones say not to give up and yet I'm so tired of the struggle. Then I'm faced with the thoughts of the possible agonies, the physical ones, and there's nothing but blackness. When I wrote the above paragraph I felt that I just couldn't possibly go any further. I just stopped writing and called Preacher Hays and went and poured out my heart which was filled with despair plus horror. I came home minus these feelings for the first time in days. If only all Christians could love more and condemn less.

March 10

Today has been a day filled with blessed peace. These times make life wonderful and precious once more. I'd begun to feel as if I'd never smile or laugh again. Once more I know prayers are going up in my behalf, and I'm so glad. I didn't go through the day just as a body. I talked with Mom tonight and for the first time in some time I felt at ease and hopeful while talking with her. With God's mighty hand Mom and Dad can once more become the trusting Christians that they have been in the past. I only pray that Rini, too, can come to grips with her problems. Everyone should read the book *Satan Is Alive and Well on Planet Earth.* We'd all be less puzzled or baffled by what goes on about us.

March 11

Once again, Lord, You've given me the night. This is the time You've given me to put the problems all away from me and accept the rest You know I have to have to keep going. I'm getting more and more tired and yet each morning I'm able to rise and face another day. This I know comes from You because I'm beyond doing for myself physically or mentally. I'm trying so hard to live just this day and no one—except someone doing it—could really know what I mean.

March 12

Each day I feel more tired, and I don't know if it's the pace I'm keeping or the treatments. I have frequent little spurts of energy that I can't explain. After I've had one it seems unreal. I should explain here that I'm really not in much pain—just drained of energy most of the time.

Sometimes I feel out of touch with God and then my world seems to crumble. I know I should turn to the Bible for comfort but for some reason I can't seem to. I told Eugene tonight that sometimes I felt as if God had forgotten me. Why am I feeling so empty so much of the time? I feel as if I'm putting on a big front. Do I really care anymore?

Was it the preacher who said you gotta love yourself before you can love your neighbor? I love myself too much to want to suffer. Right now it's taking tremendous concentration to even consider there's anyone else existing. When I'm talking to the preacher, Eugene, Marilyn and a few others, I can get beyond me but most of the time it's just me. That's when the nightmares engulf me.

Right now my body is on the bed and yet when I close my eyes it feels as if I'm floating away. I took a valium about two hours ago. Could it do that to me?

March 14

I got a note from Harriet Hanson tonight telling me that they are getting transferred to Florida. She's elated and so am I that they're going home. But, I hate to see her leave for personal reasons. She has been a source of strength to me many times this past year. I know there are, unfortunately, few Christians like her and I for one will feel the empty space. She's loved, prayed, cared for me and acted in my behalf so much. How can I adequately say "Thank You?" Even with all that, I know she won't forget me nor will I her as long as I live. Lord, I have to thank You and praise You for the privilege of knowing loving Christians like her. I count my blessings.

She wasn't and isn't alone in praying, loving, caring and acting. I'll get down frequently but I'll never completely lose sight of the greatness of my Lord who cares. I wish I could keep this in sight always. I can keep an apparently cool head most of the time. I thank God He knows and understands that once in a while I have to go to pieces, otherwise with all the pills in the world I couldn't keep going. Lord, sometimes I feel distant from You and that frightens me worse than anything. I realize that I'm the cause, but am uncertain what to do about it. I don't know exactly what to ask for but I do know I need help from You.

Tomorrow Marilyn and I will fly to Jacksonville to try to patch up a problem there. I'm asking for guidance, Lord, because I feel like I'm kinda going in blindfolded. I also request help with this business of going to the clinic. It's taking its toll once more mentally and physically. Help the trip not to exhaust me. I need all the energy I can get to stay on my feet. Ironically, if I took to the bed that would be my undoing. I'd get so stiff I wouldn't be able to move.

March 16

Thanks for everything, Lord. The trip was great. I not only didn't feel drained of energy but was able to talk and hopefully that problem is behind me. It's hard to be gloomy with Rini around. Lord, each time I go up in a plane I'm at a loss for words to explain the serenity and loveliness of being up there. I wonder about airplane pilots and those that work on the planes. Do they miss the majesty of your creation? I looked out on the ocean and once more stood amazed at such splendor.

Even with all the other problems, or perhaps because of them, I so often stand in complete awe of such love and beauty we have at our disposal. All we have to do is look and reach out. Then last and not least, all I have to do is leave home and come back to rediscover the warm and loving preciousness of home.

March 17

I weighed 113 pounds—two of that was probably water. I've felt good today and being able to come home and have everything running smoothly was wonderful. It is amazing how much better I feel. No doubt about it, Rini has a talent for organization—one day and everything is running smoothly and I can get the rest I have to have to keep going. Lord, I'm so glad You know exactly what I'm talking about. I don't even have to bother digging for words.

March 18

Another trip behind me at the clinic, or is it one of many? Lord, I guess it's a blessing that I can only take so much. I'm so thankful Rini has taken over so much of the load for me. I hate to burden others but I can't carry it alone anymore. I don't understand Mom and Dad—sometimes that depresses me almost as much as my problem.

March 21

Pat Henley took me to the clinic yesterday and that was the tenth treatment. I would like to help her but there again I don't know how. I've had trouble with my back again. It hurts most on the right side where I'm getting the treatments. I also get the shock feeling when I turn my head down.

I've come to the conclusion that I should have been an actress. It amazes me that I can carry on much as usual without any of those I work with having any idea about what's going on.

March 22

Oh, God, do you know how alone I feel? I'm sorry if I'm ungrateful but right now that's the way it is. Loved ones all around and yet how does one share death? Some might even ask "Where's your faith?" I guess I'm fresh out. Do You love me, God? Then why do I feel so empty? A year and two months is a long time to hold your breath.

Sometimes that feeling of sitting on dynamite gets to be too much and I can't handle it too well. I'd like to be real super and say I'm very ashamed of the above reaction, but I'm not. I'm human and God knows it. What I'm really thankful about is that I'm not engulfed in despair all the time. Sooner or later I'm given the peace of mind that I have to have in order to continue. Today made the eleventh treatment. Monday may be the last.

March 23

The treatments didn't end today. I get three more totaling 14. Dr. McRae assures me that the addition is good because he thinks I've responded favorably to the treatments. He also has mentioned that I'm young and strong. Strange, I feel old and run down. He also pointed out again that it would be bad if the cancer starts again. I die once more. I asked, "Can you say beyond a shadow of a doubt that this spot is cancer?" He said, "No, but with your past history we are almost sure."

Today we had severe tornado warnings and watches. I didn't hear any foul language for the first time all day at school. It's amazing how subdued people can get when they feel their own life might be in danger. People are capable of awe in regards to God's magnificence. A pity we often have to be scared out of our wits for us to take notice.

I wasn't afraid of the tornado but I have those horrors regarding cancer. If I wanted to be amusing I might say I've about worn my coffin out, climbing in and out this past year. Each time my hopes begin to grow they're snatched up by the roots. How many times can a person die mentally without dying physically also? Judging by the last 14 months I can vouch for several times.

I did get some good news today. Mom's problem should get better if she follows the doctor's instructions. It's up to her. I was afraid she'd have to have surgery.

Two more treatments and perhaps I'll never have to go through it again. If not, well, I'm no stranger to heartaches anymore, although I think I'm reaching the limit of what I can take. In all honesty I must point out that I thought I had reached that point some time back, so only God knows how much I can take. It's weird but I feel content, at ease and quite relaxed this evening. I don't often feel that way on treatment days. The Lord once more reaches out and touches in a mighty way. I'm so unworthy and yet He cares about my every feeling. I wish there were some way that I could actually help others, but I really don't know how.

Eugene goes for surgery day after tomorrow and I don't feel happy at all about that. Maybe that's crossing bridges prematurely. I can almost hear the Lord saying, "Trust Me, trust Me."

March 26

My time at home slips rapidly by. Before I know it, it's time to go back to work. I feel my good moments are from God and I feel unable to make contact. Why? I feel like I'm viewing myself from some place other than my body. It's as if I were a great actress. I see myself going through routine motions and yet I know or think it's not really me. Sometimes I think the real me has already died and only the shell remains.

James mentioned something about next Christmas and I thought, I probably won't be here. God, how can I live like this? How do I get it all together long enough to live each day without the constant thought or almost constant thought of death? I smile, laugh, talk of trivial matters, and even get into some serious conversations, and all the while I'm thinking, what does it matter? This doesn't concern me. How I do it, I don't know. Is God pleased? I doubt it, but I don't know what to do.

March 27

Preacher Hays took me to the clinic this evening. Somehow I don't think I was able to reach him. His mind was somewhere else or I couldn't make myself clear. Something was wrong. I've talked to him too many times not to know the difference. Maybe I should keep my feelings to myself. Maybe it's unfair to bog others down with my problems.

Eugene had the knot removed and I'm relieved to say it wasn't anything to be upset about. It won't do for both of us to go to pieces.

March 29

Yesterday wound up the second round of treatments. Well, Lord, what now? There are no answers from my fellow man. Isn't that right, Lord? We don't really share burdens too much, do we Lord? A few have helped but they don't have the power to help much and if they do it's only temporary. I'm so glad You've been there when it came down to the nitty-gritty. When I've cried out, only You have been able to reach out and give where I know I've really been helped. From time to time I expect from others what only You have been able to give. I suppose we can share each other's burdens but only in doing so we must realize that there's a limit to what people can do. Every time I've reached my lowest point You are the only One who pulled me out.

Later

I feel tired this evening but I enjoyed the day in general. Marilyn and family came over. She and I went shopping but cut it short because of the mobs of people that were out. Also I ran out of energy. I've had trouble with indigestion again today. Sometimes it almost feels as if my food just goes so far down my throat and stops. I even have trouble with liquids at times—it's hard to understand why. My back is sore and blistered where the treatments were given. So is my chest where it sprayed through.

My breast on the inner side also feels sore once more. The doctor and nurses didn't seem to think the treatments would cause my breast to be sore, but I think they're wrong. Last time I had treatments it made the hair on the opposite side of my head sore so why wouldn't it make my breast sore if it can blister my skin?

I felt kinda hurt with the preacher because he felt I was wallowing in self-pity when I told him how I felt. If I hadn't wanted help I'd never have mentioned how I was feeling. He seemed more interested in listening to the radio than to me or offering any help.

The Bible mentions that if a son asks for bread would his father give him a stone? I felt I was asking for help and got stone silence. I've tried to be open with him and felt that he would be the same with me. My problem isn't imaginary, physically or mentally. When I need help is it asking too much to say so? If the Preacher is the shepherd, shouldn't he be concerned when one of his flock is in real need? If he couldn't help me, couldn't he just say so?

I must expect too much. I'm a follower, not a leader and I expect leaders to lead.

March 30

We went to church today and for the first time in a long time there was nothing there for me. I couldn't respond to what the Preacher was saying because of my feelings, I suppose.

I probably never should have gone to him, much less have been as open with him as I was. I sensed a bit of uneasiness in him last Thursday and also the time before that. I don't know if it was because he didn't have the answer or if he had something else on his mind. Maybe preachers protect themselves the same as doctors. No doubt about it, I need a rest. Thank God, I have next week off.

Later

I commented to Eugene and Rini that I was beginning to resent people telling me to live one day at a time and felt that was a cop-out. Don't they realize that there are 24 hours in a day and all those hours aren't spent sleeping? Inevitably one has to think and deal with oneself. That's where I need help.

April 2

Today has been a day of rest and quiet that I needed. Thanks, Lord. I'm feeling somewhat better. I've had time to just sit, relax and read. I talked with Mom and she also sounded more relaxed than she had recently and I was very pleased to hear that. I've written several poems lately and Rini is going to check with her friend about getting them published.

April 3

Other than going to the dentist I've had a very restful day. Dr. Moon had to work on a tooth on the side of my mouth where I got the treatments. I noticed that the place where he gave the shot left a spot. The other shots didn't leave spots.

This week of rest has really been great—I needed it badly. I suppose the body can only push so much and it reaches the breaking point. I had reached that point, so once again I'm thankful.

I wrote a note of apology to Preacher Hays and after reading it he called and cleared the air. That helped a lot because I really felt terribly hurt and rejected. I must remember to come to You first, Lord, then maybe my own frame of mind will be in shape to receive help from others. I know that the business of feeling sorry for myself is a problem and that's what I feel I need help with. Is that beyond what man can help me with? If so, Lord, I'm depending entirely on You to help me over it.

I've had time to read some good books, give my thoughts to the pleasures of beautiful music, plus reading equally lovely poetry. It's really been great. Lord, when I give You a chance You really shower Your love down on me. I just need to take time to let You do what You've always wanted to do. It's really wonderful—even when my eyes and body start slipping into sleep, You're there just as You are when I awaken.

There are things I know in my heart and yet at times I begin to forget. The more I forget, the more panic-stricken I get. Forgive me for so quickly forgetting that You're right there and perfectly capable of handling any situation that arises.

There's no way words could describe how grateful I am for what Rini and Rick are doing for me. I've begun to think of Rick more as a brother instead of an in-law. I'm well aware that this isn't easy for him and yet he's totally unselfish about the matter. I'm blessed even more than I realize at times, all the more reason to be ashamed of those self-pity trips.

Days seem to slip through my hands and quickly disappear before I have a chance to fully appreciate them. Thus went my week of rest. I feel stronger and more prepared to face next week now and for that I don't forget to praise Him who made it possible. Had Rini not been here, even with the week off I wouldn't have had much rest.

April 5

Why is it difficult for people to believe me when I say, "If I'd had a choice I would have chosen not to have been born at all?" I've had a rough day.

April 6

Boy, am I slipping. I slept till 10:00 this morning. My back was hurting but has stopped now.

Later

My back is still bothering me. I can only pray that the Lord will help me make it through these last eight weeks of school. I could have used more than a week of rest. I'm still fighting this terrible tiredness. Once again my weight has dropped. Betty outweighs me by two pounds. For some reason losing weight frightens me. I can see myself shrinking to nothing. It would have been great if I'd been overweight, then I'd have been pleased with the results. Weird, huh?

Eugene, my beloved, doesn't treat me differently and Lord, I'm thankful. He did at first, but doesn't now. He's always standing by with arms to hold me when things get rough. He has strength and courage that even I never guessed at. I dare say, few men would have been as loving and patient as he's been since all this started. I'm sure his strength comes from You and I'm so thankful for You and him. It's one thing to be burdened but being without hope is quite something else. I'm blessed way beyond what I deserve even now, although there are times when I don't think about it.

April 8

Mrs. Hanson came by last night and brought encouraging reading, as usual. She is unique. I wanted to go to the ladies' meeting tonight but felt I needed the rest more.

Laura told me Monday that her fiance had been saved last Sunday night. That was really great and somewhat unusual since he comes from a Catholic background. I hope he can get into a church where he'll be able to grow as a Christian. I invited them to Zion Hill.

April 10

I've forgotten what a day without pain or discomfort feels like.

April 12

We sat up talking till 1:30 A.M. at Marilyn and Jack's last night and then spent the night. I awoke about 7:30 and soon we got it all together and came home. Eugene planted his garden and I even helped a little bit.

At the clinic today Dr. Williams said in all probability the pain was from another spot. He said that they had seen what suggested activity in the lower back where the pain started. He said I could get the X rays today or wait until the pain started again then call and they'd X ray again and start treatments again. I asked, "Does that mean that in all probability, short of a miracle, the cancer would spread all over?" He agreed.

I Thessalonians 5:18 says, "In everything give thanks: for this is the will of God in Christ Jesus concerning you." This means thank God in everything, no matter what the circumstances . . . I'll try.

April 17

I went back to work today and had a fine day, no pain, not even extremely tired! If the pain starts again then I'll go back for treatments but not until.

I'm sick and tired of being buried and given up on. Doctors are telling me in essence that it's hopeless in one breath and in the next they say they don't know. I get expressions like "Only God in Heaven knows." They and I know that only God knows so what right have they to give off with that hopeless attitude? Being around them it's next to impossible to keep a positive attitude. Why do they keep burying me before I'm dead?

Lord, You know I'm really thankful for Your presence. I've lost count of the times You've pulled me out of the depths of despair. I'm amazed at the calmness You give.

I sit there and listen to the doom that is being pronounced for my future. The doctor said he has to tell me the facts—that it's his duty, but I would have to make the decision. Only thing wrong with that is that supposedly he was telling me the facts last time and evidently not, since he saw another place also where I'd probably have trouble, later.

Lord, I love and trust You completely. Help me to make the right decisions.

April 18

Gentle breezes have caressed my day, bringing moments filled with pleasure. So many times this last year, strains of heavenly music have soothed my restless mind and body. The loveliness of different songs and instrumentals have swept me away from myself into peace indescribable. Not wasting my time on things past nor planning on an uncertain future has enabled me to be aware of *now* as I never was able to before. Perhaps that sounds drab but I know I can appreciate many things that others don't notice. I've felt just fine today once again, Lord. Thanks seem inadequate but from my heart I mean it.

I don't know if I should get the X rays, if I should just tell them everything at school or what, but please, this business of being buried frequently is beginning to wear thin.

April 19

I've stopped and found myself lost in the beauty of so many things about and above me.

So often now I hate to waste time in sleep.

Lord, You know I've fought depression today—thanks for Your help. Everything begins to feel so pointless and from there on I get into that vicious cycle of feeling helpless. Then I'm reminded that without You I am helpless.

It bothers me that Christians don't believe in miracles. I keep thinking that preachers should have more faith but everyone seems to avoid committing his faith. I know You have control of miracles but surely prayer and faith should mean something or are we supposed to pray only for people with minor problems? Isn't that putting a limit on You?

I know that sounds like I'm loading a lot on the preacher but if You call preachers to lead the people then in times of real stress what good is a leader if he doesn't believe in Your Power?

Is it ugly to think that a bothersome church member and a $1500 steeple are more important to the shepherd than a sheep who faces a real death situation? Maybe I'm being unfair.

April 20

Eugene has a rival. Pain has become my closest companion.

April 21

Strangely enough, today has been pretty good—not nearly as much pain as yesterday. The more active I am the better my back feels.

Mrs. Hanson called tonight and as always I felt so much better afterwards. I'm convinced the Lord sent her my way.

April 23

I went to the clinic for my check-up today but wasn't checked. The doctor asked if I had any more back pain and when I told him I had dull pain from time to time he suggested that I wait even for X rays. Last time he wanted me to get X rays instead of waiting. All I know is I'm glad You're there, Lord. Everyone else seems confused.

April 24

I'm not depressed—I say this because it may sound that way to anyone living in my circumstances. One of the hardest things to adjust to is the tremendous feeling of separation from almost everyone I come in contact with. In my heart I want to cry out and pour out all my thoughts and feelings, but I already know my most intense efforts would fall on deaf ears.

Doctors, counselors, preachers have all kinds of training but unless they're in the same boat how can they really know? So often I want to slip away and hide from others and myself. I know that's impossible.

I would like to give more of myself but can't right now without being completely open and then I don't know that that would be best. I've prayed about it but seem to have gotten a blank on it. It would simplify matters if the Lord would call me on the phone or write a letter.

Mom and Dad came down this evening and brought some allergy medicine for James. They both seem so much better. For that I'm glad. For a while I was wondering who would go first— them or me. They both now act like their old selves.

April 26

Sometimes I feel so determined and at other times I'm terribly tempted to just go to bed or to get in the car and start going as far as I can. I'd still be taking my biggest problem with me—me.

I asked Eugene what was I to him now and he said the question was unfair. He said that I was in his past and went on to say more. The part about the past was all that stuck in my mind. I kept thinking that to him I'm as good as dead, just like it is with other people. Lord, help me not to imagine things.

April 27

Lord, only You and I know the agony I went through just to stay at school. At times the pain was so sharp it took my breath. The pain was so bad that I was actually damp with perspiration, and for me that's unusual. I didn't go to PTA tonight but it's the first one I've missed.

I asked for Your help to get me through the day and You gave it to me. Now I need some more help to make it tomorrow. Tomorrow would be an especially bad day to miss since Amy and I are supposed to meet with Mr. Wilkins to talk over the evaluation and the possibility of being rehired. When I think back on today, once again I know I believe in miracles. Every move I made caused pain to shoot through me.

April 28

It's strange the way things work out—the evaluation was post-poned until tomorrow. Anyway, I felt much better today. It wasn't a matter of continuous pain. When I resort to the pain tablets, I've reached my limit. Last night I had begun to feel rebellious because I thought the Lord wasn't remembering that He promised He wouldn't put more on me than I could bear. Shortly afterwards the pain let up so once again I felt His loving care.

I even got to feeling well enough to go out and watch the miracle of birth. Taffy had six puppies. It's really wonderful the way animals handle birth.

April 30

My day was rough today. I felt extremely sleepy all day. Lord, You're the only one who knows how I struggle to keep going.

I kept asking myself why I put myself through all this today. I wanted to come home so much.

May 1

Mom called tonight and said her pastor read my poems and said he thought they were good and that I was talented—needless to say I was pleased.

Eugene, James and Johnny went for a weekend fishing trip. I hope they enjoy themselves and have a safe trip. Eugene needs the outlets from time to time because I realize that my problem becomes somewhat overwhelming to him and a diversion is necessary. I want him to do this but I miss him very much when he's gone.

In all honesty, at the risk of sounding dramatic, he's brought joy to my life like no other, not to mention just giving me strength to go on.

I love Betty and James dearly, but I've always felt they were temporary responsibilities—that they'd soon go their own ways and enjoy living or else give in to the not so joyous. Betty should do this with less problems because she has a lot of joy within, while James will probably have to struggle for his. I have confidence in him also because he's Eugene's son as well as mine. I hope he picks up more of Eugene's characteristics as he goes along.

May 2

Lord, I can only ask for strength for Marilyn to carry the load that has been dumped on her shoulders at this time.

May 4

Once again I find myself in the company of Mr. Pain. One of my right ribs feels extremely sore, so does my pelvic bone on the left side and my lower back. I would blame the soreness on strain but these places have hurt before. I don't know what else to think except that the cancer is probably spreading rapidly.

It's odd how I can have days, out of the blue, when I have little

117

or no pain. Sometimes I'll have a day when I find it hard to believe that anything is wrong. Friday was such a day and I felt fine all day.

I guess I'll go in tomorrow and have the X rays. I've tried to avoid going but can't keep grinding my teeth when the pain starts or rely on pain tablets. Anyway, I only have three left. If the pain got extremely bad like last Monday I might run out of tablets before Mr. Pain left. Then I'd be in agony and I'm not exaggerating.

May 5

Well, for once (or maybe a few more times than once) I was wrong. I went to the clinic this evening. They took X rays and didn't find anything except lesions. Dr. McRae said he wouldn't suggest treatments for that. He said go home and enjoy my good luck. He didn't know what caused the severe pain unless it was from strain and as to the dull ache I'd have to learn to live with that. Once again I'm convinced it's not luck but tender concern from a loving Saviour. I had asked the Lord to please take me home, then I switched and just asked for strength again. Once again, He gave me more than I asked for.

May 8

The book on the B-17 vitamin came Wednesday. This vitamin is used in other countries for cancer patients and I'm very interested in this procedure. I'm tired of the cutting, burning and poisoning methods. If I'm dying, I'd rather do it without being mutilated.

May 9

As another day draws its shades, I find myself in less pain now than I have felt earlier today. Even now I'm not completely free of it. I don't know how I'd have made out these last weeks without Rini's help. She comes to my rescue in so many ways.

I talked with Lillian Sanders this evening. She talked about not being able to talk with anybody about having cancer because no one understood: I knew exactly what she meant. In all honesty I have to admit that I count myself fortunate in that I do have several people I feel free to talk to. I'm sure out of them all she'd probably come nearer knowing the exact frustrations of the disease than most of them. She, too, treads the paths of the un-certainties that I never feel I can adequately explain to people that haven't been on the path. She understands the moment-to-moment life filled with joy to the hilt one minute then despair to the depths a second later. She understands the switching from both feelings to just not caring. The not caring is worse: that's when you want to pull your car in front of a train, slit your wrists and watch your life substance drain. The life I live astounds even me.

May 10

Mom and Dad came down for a while for our Mother's Day celebration which we had this evening. I don't think I'll go to church in the morning.

I am distressed that I no longer look forward to going to church at Zion Hill anymore. I guess I haven't forgiven Preacher Hays. I'm having trouble getting over the feeling that I was rejected, or maybe I feel that he, too, marks me off the list of the living and I'm therefore unimportant. Lord, I hate to feel that way but some-how I can't escape it.

May 11

Eugene and kids went to his Mom's after church but I stayed home to rest. I didn't go to church tonight. My back is aching but that wasn't the reason. This is a time when I need spiritual uplift, but unfortunately, right now I don't get it there. When I think of times past I could weep for I walk out of church without feeling anything. Lord, is it me?

May 12

Strange things are happening inside my body—the backaches went away but my pelvic bone felt so sore today that I had to force myself to keep from limping. If I'd limped I'd have called attention to myself and I've fought that too long to give in now with only three weeks left of school. Lord, I beg for strength to be able to finish the school year.

May 13

I had a good day with very little pain, but this evening the pain got bad and I had to take an empirin. That's the way it goes.

Pat, Ellen and the baby came up for a while. I love Pat dearly, she's such a tender-hearted person. She reminds me so much in a lot of ways of Marilyn and oddly enough of Rini, too. Rini, bless her heart, called from Marilyn's to check on me. That's love. To be encouraged all I have to do is look at those special people who surround me.

May 14

Today has been an unusually good day—very little pain today. If the Lord didn't give me some days like this I'd never make it.

My beloved went fishing. I want him to have relaxation but I worry about something happening to him.

May 15

We received a letter from the clinic in Dallas today—they were very prompt. I was disappointed that they didn't give more information. We wrote another letter asking more specific questions. Hopefully we'll get another prompt answer. Still no answer from Mexico. I'm very anxious to hear from them. I'm beginning to feel more and more frustrated—I guess that's why cancer topics are once more infiltrating my dreams.

Lord, only You know how inviting suicide is. I want to strike out at something or somebody and yet I know that it's my own body that has betrayed me. Right now I feel good physically but that's thanks to emperin.

I asked myself, "What is freedom?" I answer, "Freedom is being free to make a choice." I still have freedom to live and take a chance or take my life and not run the risk. How strong am I?

May 16

Rini called the clinic today to ask Dr. Williams to renew my prescription for the empirin, but he said he'd have to see me first. I'm furious! If I keep taking time off the job to run down there I won't have a job, much less the money to pay the vultures. Do they think I'm stupid enough to take the medicine if I don't need it? It's not as if I had a case of the measles. They, of all people, should know. I only take the tablets when I feel that I can't stand the pain anymore.

May 17

I called Dr. McRae this morning and he promptly sent in a prescription for 50 of the empirin. I thought I'd get static from him but maybe he knows a bit more about pain than Dr. Williams.

Eugene and James didn't come in tonight, although I expected them for some reason. I want Eugene to be able to relax and yet I resent him leaving me to do it. I suppose I'm selfish, but I wonder why I should feel guilty about it. His life hasn't been drastically changed by my illness, not yet anyway. He still takes his fishing, hunting and camping trips whenever he takes a notion. His spending money hasn't changed visibly—he still spends money on whatever he wants to spend it on.

When I suffer, I alone feel the pain and now most of the time when I cry, I cry alone. When I don't feel up to putting on an act I either make it a point to be alone by locking myself in my room or I force myself into putting on the act.

I lie here and listen to the rain pouring down and I can only think of the thousands who also weep. I feel very down tonight.

I talked briefly with Preacher Hays around lunch time. He said he'd talked to his doctor friend and asked about the B-17. He said the doctor wasn't too much in favor of it. He also said if he were the afflicted one he might try it or anything else. He also said he'd probably become addicted to morphine.

While we were talking someone else called him and I was more or less brushed aside. I can't help it, I feel very hurt with him and have lost the respect I once had. It's more than his attitude towards me but the way he did with a friend too.

His attitude toward me began to change after he read part of my journal. I suspect that the part where I commented that the services sometimes were rather cut and dried didn't hit too well because that was all he really even mentioned afterwards. I only suggested that the service, especially Wednesday night, was geared for those who had attended a Bible college and that I thought churches failed when it came to reaching the people. I thought so then and I still do.

Somehow, singing "Heavenly Sunlight," turning around and shaking hands with the person behind you, then walking out to go home and not caring anymore till the next service still makes me wonder about Christianity in general. I don't see anything to pat ourselves on the back for. It depresses me so to think about it I feel like throwing up my hands and quitting. Even if I had the strength, what could I do? Most of the preachers, most of the teachers, deacons, members, Christians among the congregation just don't care about one another. It's just every man for himself most of the time.

May 18

My world has righted itself. Eugene is home and once more I draw strength from him. The darkness has lifted. My beloved has that effect—strange.

May 19

I heard from the clinic in Dallas today and decided to give it a whirl. I'll probably get a lot of static but I don't see any future at all in getting cobalt till my body can't stand it anymore. Then only God knows what they would want to try. All I know is that the pain gets progressively worse. I'll be doing good to be able to finish school. Lord, I would like to know if I'm making the right decision—no letters or phone calls, huh?

May 20

If pain was measured in pounds, I'd have gained an enormous amount today. I didn't go to school until ten o'clock this morning. I could only go then because of the pain tablets. The teachers at school could never guess the physical pain I've endured in that building. When I got home I had a temperature of almost 100. I don't know what's causing that.

May 22

The pain got so bad yesterday that I got desperate and went to the clinic for more treatments. The pain stopped on the left side but I still can hardly walk due to the pain on the right side. Dear Lord, the pain I felt when James was being born was mild compared to what I've been feeling this week. A simple step has become agony.

I heard from Dr. Riddle today and going to him looks like a good idea. Let's hope it doesn't cost an arm and a leg. I hate to keep staying on the pain tablets. It begins to affect my vision, balance, appetite, and my ability to think.

May 23

I went to the clinic today for a treatment in the other leg—hopefully tomorrow I'll be able to walk better. I was running a temperature of 100 degrees this evening. Eugene called the clinic and Dr. Williams told him I was probably dehydrating and that I should be drinking two quarts of liquids a day. I think I probably drink more than that in a day because of the swallowing problem. I've found two small knots on the opposite side of my neck. I don't know if they're normal or not because my neck feels boney when nothing's wrong.

My cousin called last night to ask how I was feeling, and to encourage me about the care I'm getting by going to the clinic. I thought it was kind for him to call.

I feel as if I'm having a survival battle with death. Sometimes I embrace the thoughts of death as surely as I embrace life, but so far the reach for death is less frequent. I've stayed pretty tense and strung out for the last few days—I must watch myself. I find myself being irritable and sarcastic and no one around me deserves that.

May 31

We spent the night with Marilyn last night. I'm having on again, off again days—one I feel fair and the next, rotten. My days have become so much alike that I've got to the place where I don't want to write. I keep telling myself it could be worse. Then fear takes hold and I ask the Lord, how much worse? I try not to dwell on it but how do you get away from pain that frequently engulfs you? The left side of my neck has been bothering me—it probably has something to do with the knots I found and didn't tell the doctor about. I saw no reason to tell him unless the pain becomes unbearable because I don't plan on surgery or cobalt on that side. My ribs are also hurting a good bit, but I'll only tell when I can't take the pain anymore. Dear Lord, so often my life seems like a horrible nightmare.

June 6

All I can say is that I managed to finish up the school year without going to pieces. I look back over the last three or four weeks and wonder how. The pain tablets helped. I went to two luncheons in the last two days and both times I've listened to voices chattering and laughing about trivial matters and felt totally removed from it all, separated from most people. When I'm in the midst of situations like these I keep thinking, what a waste of time. Isn't there something better to talk about? Maybe I feel that way because I don't feel much happiness or anticipation. Many people have asked me what I plan to do during the summer. My answer should be, to try to survive or end it all.

June 15

God, why am I feeling so alone? Alone is one of the most tear-filled words to me now. I know we need to be alone at times but I always thought that meant from our fellows—not separated from God.

June 17

I measure time by how long it has been since I had a pain tablet. Dear God, how long can it go on? I've slept frequently during the day in short naps. I'm getting so weak. I'm not even sure of the date anymore, one day slips into another.

My life is naught but a fleeting shadow
slipping away.
When despair engulfs me, what can
I say?

Since tomorrow may never come,
there's no joy there,
Nor is there any consolation
in saying, it's not fair.

My very soul is drenched in tears,
My waking moments filled with
hopes slipping into fears.
Sometimes it's peace and joy more than
sorrow.
Why can't I just accept now and let
God take care of tomorrow?

June 27

I haven't been writing with any regularity because I've been much too ill. Only Eugene knows how ill.

Betty left with the Emory's to go to the mountains early this morning. I hope she has a good time. James is still at Mom's house.

June 28

Sometimes I feel so numb, so estranged from everything except pain. I keep saying to myself, "Yea, though I walk through the valley of the shadow of death, I will fear no evil for thou art with me." But sometimes I look down and the shadows close in on me and I forget You're with me, Lord, and terror engulfs me. Once again, Lord, Your presence makes me look up and give thanks for a love so precious and priceless. I can only look down for a little while and I hear the voice in my heart saying, "Look up, Robin, look up."

It's been humid and very dismal outside for the last two days. I hope for a better tomorrow.

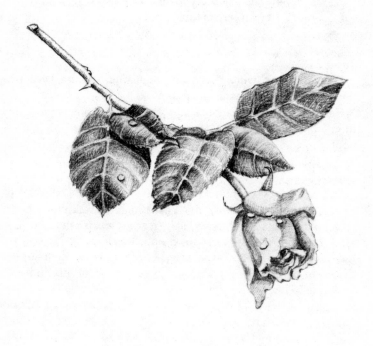

Epilogue

Hays: *Robin wrote no more. After her last entry she was hospitalized. After her hospitalization I saw her on just a few occasions. As she grew weaker she wanted more and more to be alone. Only her husband and her mother were at her side. I believe this was because she was aware of her condition and appearance. She was very sick and suffered a tremendous weight loss. I was amazed that she could deteriorate so quickly. Perhaps it was because she had spent her energy in the struggle she had made over the past year and a half.*

Eugene called one morning to let me know that Robin had slipped away to be with the Lord she loved so much. I was saddened, of course, for she had meant a great deal to me. In her notes she had said that on occasion I had been a help to her. Little did she know what a help she had been to me and my ministry. In our relationship, as her pastor and counselor I learned many things that were not taught in the seminary. Some mistakes that I made I trust never to make again. From this experience I hope to be a better listener, to have a more personal awareness of those to whom I minister, and to be a more available pastor.

Though I was saddened I was also glad. Robin had looked forward to being with the Lord. She had said, "Oh, I'll be finer all right, but whether I'll be finer here or in Heaven I don't know yet. However, Heaven will have to be finer." Well, today she is in Heaven, and I am sure she is finer—much finer.

Many others have fought this same battle. Some with the same faith and courage and some with resignation and bitterness. As far as I know, none of them has been able to share his faith and his feelings as Robin did. From the outset, she knew that the Lord was working in her life, and her desire was to be conformable to His will. She wrote these words in the front of her diary from the Amplified Bible:

> *"This is in keeping with my own eager desire and persistent expectation and hope, that I shall not disgrace myself nor be put to shame in anything; but that with the utmost freedom of speech and unfailing courage, now as always heretofore, Christ the Messiah, will be magnified and get glory and praise in this body of mine and be boldly exalted in my person, whether through life or through death." (Philippians 1:20).*

She did not disgrace herself, nor was she shamed... but she did glorify her Lord. Her testimony touched many. Her faith was contagious. Her Lord is exalted, both now and forever. Amen!